6/87

W9-CER-122

SWEATY PALMS

3

394
6

7
)

MAYWOOD PUBLIC LIBRARY
121 SOUTH 5th AVE.
MAYWOOD, ILL. 60153

SWEATY PALMS

THE NEGLECTED ART
OF BEING
INTERVIEWED

H. ANTHONY MEDLEY

TEN SPEED PRESS
BERKELEY, CALIFORNIA

TEN SPEED PRESS

SWEATY PALMS was edited and prepared for composition by Beverly Miller and Linn Fischer. Interior design was provided by Linn Fischer and the illustrations by Ken Maryanski.

©1978, 1984 by H. Anthony Medley. All rights reserved. No part of this book may be reproduced, stored in a retrieval system, or transcribed, in any form or by any means, electronic, mechanical, photocopying, recording, or otherwise, without prior written permission of the publisher, Ten Speed Press, Box 7123, Berkeley, California 94707.

Printed in the United States of America

ISBN 0-89815-139-2

Library of Congress Catalog Number: 84-24124

Additional copies of this book may be purchased from Ten Speed Press, Box 7123, Berkeley, California 94707. Please include $7.95 and an additional $1 for postage and handling.

ACKNOWLEDGMENTS

Excerpt from THE LETTERS OF F. SCOTT FITZGERALD edited by Andrew Turnbull, © 1963 Frances Scott Fitzgerald Lanahan. Reprinted by permission of Charles Scribner's Sons.
Excerpt from HOW EFFECTIVE EXECUTIVES INTERVIEW by Walter R. Mahler. Copyright © 1976 by Dow-Jones Irwin. Used by permission of Dow-Jones Irwin Company.
Excerpt from PSYCHO-CYBERNETICS by Maxwell Maltz, M.D. Copyright © 1960 by Prentice-Hall, Inc. Used by permission of Prentice-Hall, Inc.
Excerpt from MOVE AHEAD WITH POSSIBILITY THINKING by Robert Schuller. Copyright © 1967 by Robert H. Schuller. Used by permission of Doubleday and Company.
Excerpt from THE NORTHWESTERN ENDICOTT REPORT, published and copyrighted by the Placement Center, Northwestern University.
Excerpt from PERSONNEL INTERVIEWING, by Felix M. Lopez. Copyright © 1963 by McGraw-Hill Book Company. Used by permission of McGraw-Hill Book Company.
Excerpt from EMPLOYMENT PRACTICES GUIDE, published and copyrighted by Commerce Clearing House, Inc., Chicago, Illinois, and reproduced by permission of Commerce Clearing House, Inc.
Excerpt from 20th CENTURY JOURNEY by William L. Shirer, © 1977 by Simon and Schuster. Used by permission of Simon and Schuster.

For my mother
wise, gentle, strong, tender and loving

Future editions of this book will be a joint venture with you, the reader. If you have had an experience in an interview that hasn't been covered in these pages, or if you've had an experience that would serve as a good example for other interviewees, or if something bothers you that hasn't been covered here, write a letter about it to H. Anthony Medley, P.O. Box 9723, Marina del Rey, California 90295. If your letter is quoted in the next edition of this book, you'll receive a free copy of that edition.

CONTENTS

Preface

1. The Interview   1

The little things that often spell success or failure; what to bring with you; how to remember the interviewer's name; do's and dont's; how to get and retain the interviewer's attention; fact finding; control; how to assess the interviewer

2. Preparation   14

The importance of preparation; how to prepare for an interview; how to research the company; how to research the interviewer; problems with flaunting your preparation

3. Types of Interviews   23

Three types of interview styles; directed interview; nondirective interview; stress interview; group and board interviews; detailed discussion of Board interview conducted by California State Assembly

4. The Screening Interview   31

Difference between a screening and selection interview; difference between a trained and an untrained interviewer; the motivation of screening interviewer; how a screening interview works; how to conduct yourself in a screening interview

5. Enthusiasm   39

Definition of enthusiasm; importance of enthusiasm; why you should display an interest in the interview itself; categories of selling yourself; sincerity; tact; courtesy; validation; attitude; effects of taking a chance

6. The Question and the Answer   50

The feeling of the interviewer about you; interpretation of questions; the ambiguous question; the thinking pause; where to look during the interview; eye signals; the significance of each question; the blockbuster question; questions about your private life; skeletons in your closet; grievances against former employers; how to soften the effects of a possible bad reference; how to take advantage of opportunities in questions; know what you want to say and say it; how to turn questions to your advantage; the throwaway joke; dual-purpose questions

7. Assumptions 71

When "yes" doesn't mean "I agree"; unexpected reactions; how to get facts about your interviewer; false conclusions; intimidation by competition; positive thinking; disadvantages of keying your performance to false assumptions

8. Honesty 85

Effects of lying; fact versus opinion; differing interpretations; consistency; candor; how to turn an answer to your advantage without lying; elements of honesty; effects of failure to be candid with an interviewer

9. Confidence, Nervousness, and Relaxation 96

Successful people and how they handle self-doubt; how preparation can allay nervousness; how to handle the advice of others; effects of nervousness; how others handle nervousness; how to combat sweaty palms and other signs of nervousness; effects of rejection; importance of relaxation; causes of tension; how to relax; when to stop preparing

10. Dress 113

Importance of initial impressions; considerations in dressing for the interview; significance of color; effects of scents; sexy dress; how women should dress; cleanliness

11. Silence and Power 122

Use of silence by interviewers as stress; how an interviewee can use silence effectively; when not to break the silence; silence you can break and how to do so; retractions; muttering; how to endure a stressful silence calmly; silence as a plea for help; how to recognize silence being imposed as stress

12. Sex 134

How to assess what you have to offer; changing jobs; how to accept a compliment; how to evaluate the interviewer's objective; how to handle requests for dates; questions about a man's marital status; how to treat offensive questions; perils of selling sex appeal

13. Decisions 145

The halo effect; how decisions are made; methods of reaching a decision

14. Salary 151

Who should introduce the subject; how to know yourself; desires versus requirements; how to treat questions about your compensation; how to handle vacation

15. Discrimination 164

Federal and state laws; unlawful questions; how to respond to an unlawful question; conciliation; attorneys; how to file a lawsuit yourself; remedies; damages; liability of state and local governments

Bibliography 188

As Gertrude Stein lay dying in the July heat of 1946 in Paris she mumbled to someone by her bedside: "What is the answer?" And when there was no answer she said: "Then what is the question?"

—William L. Shirer

PREFACE

Fantastic! After months of sending out résumés and making telephone calls, you finally have an interview. You're excited and feel that your long search is over.

But then exhilaration may dampen. You feel a vague uneasiness, which you have no trouble tracing to nervousness and fear. In trying to get your interview, you've been dealing with basically inanimate objects—preparing résumés, talking into one end of the telephone, writing letters. But now you've got to perform. You're going to meet a person face to face for an extended period of time, and you realize that a decision will be made on you from that meeting.

What do you do? How can you prepare? What will the interviewer ask? What should you say? What should you wear? What can you ask him? These and hundreds of other questions come flooding to your mind. My God, you think, I've got to find something out about what's going to happen.

So you go to the library—and find nothing. All the books available have been written on how to find a job. They are basically books on how to **get** an interview, not how to **conduct** yourself in that interview. Next you ask placement counselors—and their answer that you should just follow your interviewer's lead doesn't relieve you. So you get more and more nervous and go to the interview cold, planning to play it by ear. You figure that the interviewer will ask what he wants to ask, and all you have to do is answer his questions.

Still you feel uneasy. There must be more to it than that, you worry. But since you can't find any books on the subject, and your counselors seem to think that all you have to do is answer the interviewer's questions, you let it go at that and do nothing more to prepare. This feeling is buttressed if you have taken the time to read any of the books on how to find a job. These books devote page after page to how to write a résumé, how to decide what you want to do, who to go to to find a job, who to go to for counseling, and so on. These books are basically books on how to get an **interview,** not how to get a job.

Since getting an interview is difficult (it has been reported that of many different companies studied, one invitation to interview is made for every 245 resumes received), it is appropriate to devote a great deal of time and thought into getting in the door.

But then all the advisers, counselors, and writers just leave you there. What happens now? Well, since there isn't anything much written on it, it must just be up to the interviewer to ask what he wants. So you timidly enter the interview alone and totally unprepared.

In my profession as an attorney, I've interviewed hundreds of people for positions—from lawyers to secretaries and other positions. In my business of operating a videotaped interview service for major law firms throughout the country, I've interviewed thousands of law students. Two things stand out from these interviews: most knew nothing about the interview process, and most had a yearning to learn more about it but didn't know where to start.

That's how this book was born. It was not unusual for law students I interviewed to ask me questions about their technique after we finished. Since I did not make a hire-no hire decision on them, they viewed me as an objective person who could give them sound advice. When these questions became the rule rather than the exception, I felt that it would aid me if I could recommend some books for them to read. But after scouring many libraries, bookstores, and *Books in Print*, I discovered that there was nothing written on the subject. In order to fill that void, this book resulted.

Fear of the unknown is one of the primary causes of nervousness in an interview. This book will help by telling you:

□ what an interview is

□ the various types of interviews

□ how to allay your fears

□ how to control the content of the interview

□ how to present yourself in the best light

□ how to parry tough questions

□ how to keep from offending the interviewer

□ how to prepare for an interview

□ how to relax

- how to dress
- how to counteract the effects of a bad reference
- how to turn questions to your advantage
- how to handle stress
- how to handle salary discussions
- what the law prohibits an interviewer from asking
- how to enforce your legal rights

THE INTERVIEW

A candidate I once interviewed for a secretarial position could type 90 words per minute and take shorthand at 120 words per minute. She was attractive and presentable and had good references. But after showing up ten minutes late, she called me "Mr. Melody" throughout the interview.

The two main things I remembered about her were that she had kept me waiting and had constantly mispronounced my name. I finally offered the position to someone whose typing and shorthand skills were not nearly so good.

More often than not, it is the small things that occur in an interview that spell the difference between getting an offer and being rejected. As you will learn as you read on, the basic objective of a candidate in an interview is to spark a positive feeling in the interviewer. It's a purely subjective feeling, so your close attention to the little things is essential.

▶ The basics

Be certain of the time and place of the interview and the name of the interviewer. Sometimes candidates are so excited to get an interview that they neglect to ask for this essential information. Write it down and keep it with you until after the interview. If no one tells you your interviewer's name, ask. Sometimes the situation precludes finding out, but you're ahead of the game if you know it going in.

Arrive early for the interview. If you plan on arriving at least fifteen minutes before the appointed time, you will have a cushion against any unforeseen delays, such as a traffic tie-up or an elevator breakdown or an inability to find the right building or office, any of which could cause you to be late if you depended on split-second timing. Being early can also give the interviewer a good initial impression of your reliability and interest.

Bring a pen and notebook with you. The notebook should fit in a pocket or purse so that you don't walk into the interview room with it in hand. Its purpose is twofold. First, the interviewer may give you some information for you to write down. If you're prepared with your own writing material, it will save him from trying to find something for you during the interview.

☞ *Second, immediately after the interview you should write down what occurred: what you said, what he said, and what your reactions were to him. This information can be very important in future interviews so that you can be sure that what you tell the interviewer is consistent. Further, if you have many different interviews, your notes of each will help your recall of each and aid in making a choice in jobs, should that become necessary. Don't, however, make notes during the interview unless the interviewer asks you to write something down.*

Remember the interviewer's name. There is possibly no sweeter sound to the human ear than the sound of one's own name. If you don't know the interviewer's name prior to meeting him, concentrate on it when he introduces himself and remember it. For some people this is very difficult. They are concentrating on themselves so much and thinking about how nervous they are that they completely forget the name or don't pay close attention when they hear it for the first time.

When he introduces himself, repeat his name immediately by saying something on the order of, "How do you do, Mr. Smith." Then repeat the name a couple of times during the first part of the interview. This repetition will help you to remember the name. It will also have a pleasing effect on the interviewer, who undoubtedly likes to hear the sound of his name.

One caveat: do not call the interviewer by his or her first name unless invited to do so (something that is very unlikely). Calling people by their first name without being asked is a familiarity that offends a great many.

Remember Christ's parable comparing the guest at a wedding feast who sat near the head of the table and was embarrassed by being asked to move farther down with the guest who sat at the lowest place and was honored by being asked to move up. You have nothing to lose by calling your interviewer "Mr., Ms., Miss" or "Mrs." and nothing to gain by calling your interviewer "Charlie" or "Shirley." If your interviewer is a woman, notice whether she's wearing a wedding ring. If not, I recommend calling her "Ms." If she's sympathetic to the women's movement, it could be a plus for you, whereas calling her "Miss" may offend her. On the other hand, if she is not sympathetic to the women's movement, calling her "Ms." should not offend her as much as calling her "Miss" could offend one who is sympathetic.

Don't offer to shake hands unless the interviewer offers a hand first. I was raised by my mother to obey the old rule of polite society that a gentleman does not offer his hand to a lady unless she offers her hand first. But as an interviewer, I always offer to shake hands, whether the interviewee is male or female. I am initially trying to put the interviewee at ease, and a handshake is a good way to break down some barriers.

But interviewers are different. Some will not offer to shake hands. A male interviewee should not offer to shake hands if his interviewer does not first offer. For a woman, this is not so crucial. You may find a chivalrous interviewer who believes it is offensive for a man to offer his hand to a woman but would not be offended for a female interviewee to offer her hand to him. The safe rule, in any event, is not to offer your hand unless the interviewer makes the first move.

If you do shake hands, make it a firm grip. A weak handshake can be a real turnoff. But don't go overboard and show your Charles Atlas grip. If you break a few bones in his hand or bring him to his knees by your hearty handshake, he won't remember you with good feelings.

Don't smoke unless invited. Many people are allergic to cigarette smoke. Further, the interviewer may have to occupy the room for the entire day, and he doesn't want it filled up with smoke. Smoking has generally become so controversial that you shouldn't take the chance on offending him by lighting up without being invited. No matter how addicted you are to tobacco, you should be able to survive a few minutes without your dose. Many nonsmokers have an almost religious antagonism to smoking. Why risk offending?

Don't chew gum. Gum chewing can communicate a distinctly negative impression. It may not offend some interviewers, but it is still better not to take the risk of doing something that may rub him the wrong way.

Wait for your interviewer to sit down or offer you a chair before seating yourself.

Most of these suggestions are items of common courtesy, but they are often overlooked, particularly in the context of the interview when you are nervous and thinking about yourself.

☞   *If there is ever a time to think of the other person, the interview is that time.*

It is a keystone of any effective interview for you to come across as an honest person. "Here I am with all my warts" is the impression that is best to leave. You don't want to expound on your warts, but you want to leave the impression that you accept yourself for what you are and that you want the interviewer to know you as the person you are.

But that's just the *impression* you want to leave. You must attune yourself to the interviewer early, and this requires strict attention to him and his reactions to you.

You will have to make some very astute judgments in the early moments of the interview about the interviewer. In order for you to conduct an effective interview, you must concern yourself with the interviewer's problems, prejudices, desires, and feelings. Is he dynamic, a take-charge guy who wants to regale you with stories? Let him. Is he somewhat shy and insecure in his position? Help him out. Does he exhibit any prejudices that you are able to perceive? Don't run afoul of them.

You must exercise the perception to categorize him early and then the discretion to guide the interview along the lines that help him arrive at the conclusion you wish.

Being interviewed and being interviewed well are two entirely different matters.

▶ You must sell yourself

As an interviewee you are primarily a salesman. The product you are selling is yourself, and the assets of the product consist of your experience, skills, and personality. You communicate your experience and skills in your résumé. Your personality comes across in the interview.

You must recognize that you are in a selling situation and that it is your goal to arouse the interest of the interviewer in you. If you wait expectantly for his questions and dutifully answer them, you have done nothing to distinguish yourself from the hundreds of other interviewees he will encounter.

Paul Ivey, in his classic *Successful Salesmanship*, states, "There is one sure-fire way of arousing [their] interest . . . : find out what they are already interested in and then talk about it. If you talk about what they are interested in, they will later on be willing to consider what you are interested in."

Boredom is an invariable element of interviewing. If you add to the boredom, you're putting nails in your coffin. Shortly after John F. Kennedy was elected president, he had decided upon a farm leader to be his secretary of agriculture and invited the candidate to his Georgetown apartment for an initial interview. "It was so boring," he said later, "and the living room was so warm, that I actually fell asleep." The candidate was quickly rejected.

An interviewer will ask the same questions of people with similar interests and backgrounds and receive the same answers. One of the better techniques of good interviewing is to break that boredom and routine by getting the interviewer to talk about something that interests him. If the time is right and the interviewer seems receptive, you can do this by inquiring, "Gee, you must get awfully tired of interviewing for this position. What do you do to break the monotony?"

☞ *You should be outwardly oriented. You should think about the interviewer and gear the interview toward his concerns. If you talk intelligently about something in which he is concerned, he will be more interested in the areas of your concern. Interviewers are like everyone else: they are selfish, and their own concerns are paramount in their minds. If you show a genuine interest in them and can discuss them intelligently, the interest in you will be sparked. If, on the other hand, you are unable to communicate your interest with sincerity, the likely consequence will be a loss of confidence in you, and you'll be worse off than when you started.*

▶ Keep the interviewer's attention

☞ Pay strict attention to how you are being received by the interviewer. If you determine that his interest is lagging, there are a few tricks you can use to bring him back around.

You can vary the tone of your voice (for example, by lowering it or making it louder). Television advertisers often do this by making their commercials louder than the show they sponsor. Theoretically this change in tone beckons and makes the viewer more attentive to something he may have little desire to hear.

You can vary the tempo at which you speak (by speeding it up or slowing it down). Essentially any change that you make from the manner in which you had been behaving will act as a lure to bring the interviewer's attention back from its wandering. You must capture and retain the interviewer's interest, or the remainder of the interview will be a mere formality and probably result in rejection.

What you do with that attention once you capture it will determine whether your interview is going to be successful. If, for example, you convince the interviewer that you don't have the experience for the job or the skills required or that your personality is abrasive or bland, you're no better off than you were before you walked in the door.

Once you have captured his attention, you must continue *your salesmanship and create the desire in the interviewer to have you as an employee.*

Paul Ivey says that "desire . . . rests on conviction; and the former cannot be created without the latter. . . . The intelligent salesman adjusts his sales talk to the customer's system of beliefs; his ideas enter the customer's mind unpercepted because they are so similar to the customer's own ideas. There is no customer-resistance, but rather customer-assistance. There is agreement instead of disagreement." Your preparation and perception thus become important bases. If you have researched the interviewer (in ways discussed in the next chapter), you know enough about him to make some initial judgments as to what kind of person he is. If you know his background and what he's done, you may be able to make some intelligent guesses as to his beliefs. But before you act on these assumptions, you must make some evaluations during the initial part of the interview.

▶ Fact finding

If you can get the interviewer to talk about himself or reveal something personal in an early part of the interview, you can reinforce or verify some of your assumptions before you act on them. The first part of the interview can be a jousting period while you feel him out and vice versa. What you must realize is that he has probably assumed that you are the typical interviewee who will meekly sit and wait for him to conduct the interview. Therefore, he will not be prepared for subtle probes.

☞ *You must take your key from him. If he starts boldly by asking questions and gives you no signal that he will entertain personal queries, you have to wait until the time is propitious.*

If you are unable to penetrate his shield, you can still work on some existing beliefs you may safely assume that he has from interpreting his actions. For example, if you have submitted your résumé in advance and then been called in for an interview, you may safely assume that the interviewer has made a preliminary determination that you are qualified for the position based upon the data you provided. You may then proceed to work upon this belief by verifying and amplifying the facts on your résumé and by detailing specific experience and skills.

You can also assume that the interviewer knows what he wants out of the position, and you may query him on how he views the position and the tasks he wants accomplished. After he has discussed this, you can tailor your experience and skills to the desires he has revealed.

☞ **It's important that you get from him some kind of a job specification early in the interview so that you can key what you can accomplish to what he wants accomplished.** If you get into a detailed discussion of your skills and experience before you've had a chance to probe what he's looking for, you're adrift in a world of unknowns.

Some interviewers will tell you something about the job before they start questioning you, but most won't. Most interviewers are inwardly oriented, just as are most interviewees, and they may not really focus on the interviewee. They may be thinking instead about asking the right questions in the interview.

Therefore if you can easily segue into questioning him about the position early on, he may give you some valuable keys that you can use to guide the rest of the interview and create in him the realization that you are the right person to fill the position.

▶ When he sees himself in you

If you can strike a responsive chord in the interviewer by ☞ having him conclude that the two of you think alike, you will have gone a long way toward creating the feeling in him that can result in an offer, as the following incident illustrates.

Robert A. Lovett was described by David Halberstam in *The Best and the Brightest* as "the symbolic expert, representative of the best of the breed . . . a man of impeccable credentials, indeed he passed on other people's credentials, deciding who was safe and sound, who was ready for advancement and who was not." Charles B. (Tex) Thornton was the founder, chairman of the board, and chief executive officer of Litton Industries, the pioneer conglomerate, a man of immense wealth and power, and at one time the nominal chief of staff of the captains of industry in the United States.

One day these titans met for the first time. Lovett was assistant secretary of war in 1941 and Thornton was a twenty-seven-year-old, $4,600-a-year statistician for the U.S. Housing Authority in Washington. Young Thornton had written a report that had interested Lovett, and Lovett wanted to meet Thornton. Thornton telephoned for an appointment and found himself waiting impatiently in Lovett's outer office. Willing to wait no longer, he rose to leave, when Lovett's secretary persuaded him to wait a few minutes longer, an act that Thornton has said changed the whole course of his life.

After Lovett arrived he and Thornton talked. The more the youthful Thornton spoke, the more Lovett liked him. Lovett was a banker who had a love affair with figures and Thornton talked of numbers as if they were a language of their own. This impressed Lovett immensely. Here was a man in his own mold! Not only that, but Thornton was not intimidated by Lovett's authority. Lovett was looking for just such a person.

Thornton was prepared. He spoke the technical language, and he revealed that he knew what he was talking about. He was respectful of the man and the office of Lovett but communicated his respect in himself so that he was not obeisant. He was not intimidated by Lovett or his office. He met Lovett as an intellectual equal, while deferring to the office and experience of the older man. Thornton ignited a feeling in Lovett and Lovett hired him. From that point, Thornton was associating with the powers that ran the World War II logistical effort. He built a reputation that enabled him to negotiate a lucrative contract for himself and several colleagues with Hughes Aircraft after the war and finally left Hughes to found Litton and his own fortune. He traces his success to this interview with Lovett. Had he not impressed Lovett sufficiently the world may never have heard of Tex Thornton.

Lovett later said that Thornton reminded him of himself in the way he spoke about figures. Thornton came across in the interview as a man of unusual intellectual capability, but having Lovett identify so personally with Thornton was the essential element in the entire interview.

 If you can make an interviewer see another him in you, you will have won him over.

Lovett saw that Thornton thought as he did and identified with him. Without question, Lovett made a conclusion based upon the "halo" effect of this feeling. (The halo effect is discussed in chapter 13.) Thornton continued to perform, but this one impression that he created during the interview got him his chance.

▶ Control

An interviewer can be expected to control the flow of the interview.

Some interviewers may begin by asking general questions to ease your nervousness and will then move on to more specific questions about areas in which they are interested that are not covered on your résumé.

 But although the interviewer controls the flow of the interview, the interviewee controls its content.

After all, an interview generally consists of an interviewer's asking questions and the interviewee's answering them. What the interviewee does with the questions is up to him. Thus you should go into the interview knowing the points that you want to cover, for example, your achievements.

▶ Think about the interviewer

Don't think about yourself so much. Most interviewees think about themselves to the exclusion of everyone else. When you walk into a room, you may be worrying about how you look, whether your palms are sweaty, whether your voice will crack.

But we all think about ourselves. The interviewer is thinking about **himself.** Maybe he doesn't have the same insecurities attacking him, but he's thinking about himself all the same. He may be worried about his job or making the plane that night. Or maybe he's worried about his ill child or that his wife (her husband) is in bed with another man (woman) or an argument he had with his boss. He may have a million things on his mind other than this interviewee sitting in front of him.

So there you are worrying about yourself and your sweaty palms and there he is thinking about something else. In fact the interviewer may have the same insecurities. He may not have conducted many interviews and be worried that he's going to make a fool of himself. He may even be worried that **his** palms are sweaty or that he won't ask the right questions. Or, worse, if he is really inexperienced, he may feel that he won't be able to think of anything to say and there will be gaps of silence.

Whatever his thoughts, there's a good possibility that he's not thinking what you think he's thinking. He's **not** taking you apart piece by piece in his mind, coolly evaluating your every movement.

It's your responsibility to think about him.

If you determine that he is insecure and unsure of himself, try to make the interview go as smoothly as possible for him. If you do and you control the interview to the extent that there are no gaps and you say what you want to say, you will have probably conducted a very good interview.

☞ *If you go into the interview thinking about the interviewer, you will relieve yourself of the tremendous tension that most interviewees feel about an interview. You will feel that you have some control of the situation and a plan of attack.*

As a student I once entered an interview room at the end of a warm spring day, and the interviewer was standing with his back to me staring out the window. It was obvious that he was bored to tears. He had had twenty-five interviews with students who were carbon copies of one another, and he had a few more to go of the same monotonous questions and answers.

I had just heard some news on the radio, so before he could start into his routine of questions, I asked, "Did you hear that Khrushchev was overthrown?"

His eyes lit up, and we spent several minutes talking of Russia, which we had both visited. Suddenly his routine was broken, and right off the bat we had something in common. I was invited to see his firm and, although I didn't take a job with them, the interview was a success because I thought about breaking his boredom rather than worrying about whether my pants were pressed.

You have to take the key from the interviewer. If he is relaxed, self-confident, and interested, you don't have to worry too much about bringing him out of himself. But if you can get him to talk about himself with interest, you will have several advantages. First, he'll reveal quite a bit about himself, giving you information you can use as the interview progresses. Second, everyone likes to talk about themselves and if you're interested and communicate that interest, the feeling you're trying to create in him will be enhanced. Third, you'll have a better chance to find areas of common interest and areas of possible conflict to avoid.

If you get the chance, ask him personal questions. Is he married? Does he have children? Does he play tennis? Does he listen to Bach, Neil Diamond, or the Rolling Stones? Has he ever been to Katmandu? If you can discover something in common, you will be way ahead of the game.

Some interviewers can react negatively to such probing, so you have to do it in a natural, conversational way. But just think. How would you feel if the highlight of your life was when you ice-skated on the Bering Straits and suddenly you're interviewing someone who did the same thing. Would you be inclined to offer her a job? Is Raquel Welch round?

CHECKLIST

★ Write down the time and place of the interview and the name of the interviewer.

★ Arrive early for the interview.

★ Bring a pen and notebook with you.

★ Write a synopsis of the interview immediately afterward.

★ Remember the interviewer's name.

★ Don't offer to shake hands unless the interviewer offers a hand first.

★ Don't smoke unless invited.

★ Don't chew gum.

★ Wait for the interviewer to sit down or offer you a chair before you sit down.

★ Present yourself as an honest person; do not try to hide anything.

★ Remember you're selling yourself.

★ Remember to combat the interviewer's boredom.

★ Be outwardly oriented.

★ Retain the interviewer's attention by varying the tempo of your speech and the tone of your voice.

★ Get the interviewer to talk about himself early.

★ Get him to give you a job specification early in the interview.

★ Remember your goal is to strike a good feeling in him about you.

★ You must control the content of the interview.

★ Don't think about yourself so much.

★ Recognize the insecurities of the interviewer.

2

PREPARATION

A hit Broadway show consists of two and a half hours of entertainment, which is the culmination of endless weeks of rehearsal and hard work to prepare the finished performance. A ballerina started taking lessons at the age of six to accomplish that pirouette that seems so effortless when she's twenty-one. The basketball player started shooting baskets when he was nine to perfect that jumpshot he nets with seeming ease when he's twenty-five.

If we want to do something well, we spend a disproportionate amount of time preparing for it compared with the time it takes to do the actual deed. Being interviewed should be no different. The typical interviewee will spend hours and hours to get an interview, but once she gets it she figures that the interview will take care of itself. Beyond getting up in the morning and perhaps dressing a little better than she normally would, she won't spend any further time or effort preparing for it.

The reason interviewees act this way is based upon the misperception that the interviewer will know exactly what he wants to get out of the interview and will ask the questions he needs in order to arrive at the answers he seeks. Thus, the interviewee thinks, what can I do to prepare? I don't know what he is looking for. I'll just go to the interview and answer his questions.

Unfortunately the vast majority of interviewees don't realize that it is up to them to control the content of the interview. Remember that you are the salesman and the product you are selling is yourself. You should not leave it up to the interviewer to probe wildly for areas of concern. If you're savvy, you'll gently lead the interviewer to your strengths. The primary element in controlling the interview is to be prepared.

▶ Research the company

Learn as much as you can about the company you will be interviewing. If you were a salesman, you wouldn't dream of going into a sales presentation without knowing something about the business of the potential customer. You would tailor your sales pitch to the needs of that business. If you were going to make a speech, you would want to know as much about the audience as you could so that you could direct your speech to the areas of the audience's interests. Similarly, when you go into an interview, you should know as much about the company as possible so that you can train your approach toward making the interviewer feel that you fit the requirements of the job.

The impression left by your preparation is sometimes subtle, but it is invariably positive. If, for example, you are interviewing a bank and have a working knowledge of what the bank does, this knowledge will come across to the interviewer. Conversely, if you are ignorant of the bank's business, it will register as a definite negative.

☞ Interviewers are looking to determine not only your interest in obtaining a job but in working for their company, rather than some other one. If you've taken the initiative to find out what the company does, it indicates that you have done some homework. If you don't have the interest to find out what kind of work the company does prior to the interview, that lack of interest may be quickly discovered by the interviewer. Not only can you expect to be thrown for a loss by some questions asked by the interviewer, but he may draw a distinctly negative impression from your apparent lack of interest.

One prime question you can expect is what you think you can add to the company as an employee. How can you answer that if you don't even know what the company does? Whether you have done this basic amount of research will come out in other ways. For example, most interviewers will reach a point where they ask you if you have any questions about the company or its operations. This may seem to be a maneuver to turn the interview over to you, but in fact it's a very potent question. From the questions you ask, the interviewer can determine how much you know of the company and for what reasons, if any, you would like to work for it.

▶ How to research the company

How do you research the company? College placement offices are ideal repositories of information. They are generally responsive to requests for information, whether or not you are a student or alumnus, although their policies differ in accordance with the personality of the person running the office. They are good places to start, and if the inquiry does result in rejection, you haven't lost anything.

There is a myriad of publications to which you may refer. Some of these include:

Better Business Bureau reports
Chamber of Commerce publications

College Placement Directory (Zimmerman & Lavine)
College Placement Annual (College Placement Council)
Dun & Bradstreet Reference Book
Fitch Corporations Manuals
Moody's Manuals
MacRae's Bluebook
Poor's Register of Directors and Executives
Standard & Poor's publications
Thomas' Register of American Manufacturers
annual reports
For public companies, documents required to be filed with the
    Securities Exchange Commission, such as registration state-
    ments and the annual report form (10-K).

Placement offices should also have other printed material on companies that recruit at their school.

Stock brokers may know something about the company and its personnel. College professors who teach subjects in the field of the company's line of work may be helpful. You can anonymously contact the company's public relations department and get quite a bit of information about the company.

A less traditional avenue is to find the cocktail lounge near the company's offices where the workers go after work and drop in for a drink at quitting time. If you can strike up a conversation with a secretary, you will be close to a source of gossip that can provide you with the up-to-date talk of the employees within the company. You can check out that information with your other sources. A visit like this can help you gather data in preparation for your interview and give you a valuable insight into the company and its morale. It can help you to make a judgment on the company and determine how happy you would be working in such an environment.

If you know the name of your interviewer, you can make discreet inquiries about him by dropping his name. This can be a dangerous tack, however, because it could get back to him. Asking someone, "Do you know Jack Spratt?" can elicit affirmative responses. If it does, however, you don't want the person with whom you're speaking to go to Spratt and mention that you were asking about him—so make it clear that you don't know him personally. Saying "my brother-in-law knows him" or some similar disclaimer can protect you against this risk.

Once you've found someone who knows him, try dropping an innocuous, "I hear he's really doing well." This is a meaningless comment, but it can result in starting your partner on a personal discussion of Mr. Spratt, and your knowledge will be rapidly expanded. This technique is offered with the disclaimer that if the interviewer discovers that you were doing a background check on him, he may be offended. No one likes to have someone probing about him, even if your intentions are all the best. So if you are inclined to go to this much trouble, be aware that it could backfire and ruin your interview before you walk in the door. If you're not excited by James Bond snooping in someone's file drawers in the dim of night with a flashlight and footsteps coming down the hall, this may not be for you.

If your interview has been arranged by an executive search firm or a placement agency, you can probe the search consultant for information. The consultant will have already done a preliminary check on you and will probably have held an interview to prescreen you. He is placing his reputation on the line by recommending you for an interview, so he wants you to look as good as possible. Ask him as many questions as you want about the company and the person who will be interviewing you. The consultant will tell you as much as he can. You are money to him. If his client offers you a job and you accept it, he gets a big fee, so he's trying his best to make a marriage.

 What information do you want on the company? First, of course, you want to know what it does. Is it a conglomerate? What areas is it in? What does it manufacture? What does it sell? Does it perform services? What services? Is it making money? Is the profit trend up or down? Is it expanding or contracting? What are its prospects?

You will also want to know about the area where the open job is. The same questions you ask about the company can be asked about the division in which you may be working.

◆ Learn about the product

If there's a product involved, learn about the product. When I first took a job as a young attorney for Litton Industries, I was interviewing for the position as an assistant division counsel for their Guidance & Control Sytems Division. That name alone was enough to boggle my mind. A scientist I was not. After a little research, I found that they made something called an inertial navigation system. That was worse than the name of the division. What was an inertial navigation system?

Finally I went to a fraternity brother who had majored in engineering and asked him if he knew what it was all about. He explained to me that inertial navigation was a method of navigating whereby the system allows you, if you know your starting point, to measure speed and distance and therefore know where you are at all times. He also explained the components of the system.

When I went into my interview with the division counsel, I astounded him by my ability to talk the jargon of inertial navigation. Of course I didn't understand it then, nor do I now, but I exhibited at least a modicum of intelligence about the subject.

He later told me that I was the first person he had interviewed for the job to whom he did not have to explain inertial navigation. Since he didn't understand it any better than I did, his being relieved of this obligation was a big plus in my favor. Also he said that he knew that it was not an easy task for me to find someone who could explain the subject and to understand it well enough to have the confidence to discuss it. My initiative and interest in going to this extent to prepare for the interview impressed him.

So few people have the interest or drive to do this amount of work preparing for an interview. If you do, and if you learn about as mystifying a product as an inertial navigation system, you should have a big advantage over your competition.

▶ Find out about the interviewer

You should discover as much as you can about the person who will be conducting the interview. Where was he born? Where was he educated? What's he done that's unusual? What's his area of expertise?

An interviewer sometimes will try and get inside you, perhaps by asking you questions involving some controversy.

While most often these questions are asked to determine your thought patterns rather than your positions on issues, if you have a general feel for the interviewer, it can save you from voicing a dogmatic opinon that would offend him and result in your rejection. If the interviewer was a marine colonel in Vietnam, you probably would want to avoid voicing sympathy for the draft resisters living abroad. Or if the interviewer is Jewish, you may decide to play down your admiration for Yasir Arafat. If he is an active member of the local American Civil Liberties Union, you may not want to emphasize your support of preventive detention.

If you can learn something about the person who is going to interview you, you can steer clear of sensitive areas and concentrate on discussing things that you may have in common.

Further, you will have a much better chance to bring the interviewer out of himself. If you can get an interviewer to discuss some personal aspect of his life, you will have broken through a barrier. **In order to receive an offer, an interviewee wants to have the interviewer come out of the interview with the feeling, "I really liked that person."** If you know something about the interviewer, you are better able to affect the flow of the interview and keep on topics where you won't offend. You may even get him to depart from the relatively impersonal format of a selection interview and discuss with you an aspect close to him and his life.

▶ Don't flaunt your preparation

Many interviewees make the mistake of flaunting their preparation in the interview. They want to make sure that the interviewer is aware of the fact that they had so much interest in the job that they devoted a lot of time to researching and preparing for the interview. This can come across as insincere. The reason that you do the preparation is to make yourself ready for the interview by learning about the company and the person conducting the interview. But you want this information so that you can make an intelligent decision. If you did the preparation only to impress the interviewer with your knowledge and he perceives this, it will be a negative factor.

Interviewers can spot interviewees who are acting in a "programmed" manner, rather than naturally. If the interviewer feels that the interviewee is playing a game with the interview, it will rapidly turn from a selection interview into a rejection interview. Joseph Alibrandi, president and chief executive officer of Whittaker Corporation, says, "If there's one thing in an interview that's important to me, it's that I see the real person, not some guy who's playing a role that some search consultant has advised him on—how to sit and how to talk and all that—because I see through that in five minutes and it's pathetic."

If you've done your research and preparation, it'll come across to the interviewer in the natural course of the interview. You will convey possession of knowledge and information through your demeanor and reactions to questions. If it comes across naturally, the reaction will be positive.

Don't make the mistake of asking a question for the sake of the question itself. Alibrandi says, "Many times guys will ask questions because they think it's intelligent and it satisfies some requirement that somebody set up for the kinds of things you should know about a company. When somebody asks a question like that, I think that he's asking that for my benefit. If that was really important to him he could have found it out by looking at the annual report. It gives you a feel for the kind of person he is. You feel that he can't separate the cosmetics from the fundamentals. I'm amazed that he's sitting with me and really believes that that cosmetic is going to help him. It would be a real negative because what you're really looking for are the basic traits, honesty, ability to work with people, ability to relate to people."

Ernest Hemingway developed a way of writing in which he would write a story and then omit several pages at the beginning, theorizing that something omitted can affect the reader as if it were there. He used this method in several of his short stories and in his first novel, *The Sun Also Rises*. This same theory applies to an interviewee's preparation. Even though you do not discuss all you know about the company and the person conducting the interview, you will convey a sense of knowledge during the interview. Your knowledge obtained through your preparation, even though unstated, will have a presence and will affect the interview and the feeling developed by the interviewer.

☞ *Just as a person with power doesn't have to say, "I am powerful," you don't have to say, "I know a lot about you and your company." The powerful person radiates power. The knowledgeable person radiates knowledge. To discuss it, to bring it out in the open for no reason is to diminish it and to turn a plus into a negative.*

CHECKLIST

★ Preparation is the key to achievement.

★ Don't go into the interview thinking that the interviewer knows exactly what he wants out of the interview and will ask the appropriate questions.

★ The interviewer will control the **flow** of the interview.

★ You must control the **content** of the interview.

★ You are selling yourself.

★ Learn as much as you can about the company you're interviewing.

★ Interviewers want to know specifically why you are interested in their company.

★ One question to expect is, "What can you add to our company as an employee?"

★ Learn about the product or service the company manufactures, sells, or performs.

★ Learn about the interviewer.

★ Don't ask questions for the sake of impressing your interviewer with the question itself.

★ Don't flaunt your preparation.

3

TYPES OF INTERVIEWS

The word **interview** is derived from the French **entrevue, entrevoir** ("to see one another," "meet"). Although generally the term applies to job applicants (for instance, Webster's defines it as "a formal consultation usually to evaluate the aptitude, training or progress of a student or prospective employee"), it should not be so limited. An interview includes any confrontation between two people when the understood purpose is for at least one of the two to make an evaluation of the other **for any reason.** Thus, a meeting between a general contractor and a subcontractor for bidding evaluation is an interview. A meeting between a client and an attorney whom the client is considering retaining is an interview. Any time one meets with another for the purpose of making a judgment on that other person, an interview is occurring.

Although the vast majority of positions are filled through interviews by supervisors totally untrained in the scientific approach to interviewing, the well-prepared candidate will have a knowledge of the various types of interviews with which he might be faced.

 It is always advisable in any endeavor to approach it as if you are going to be faced with a conscientious, knowledgeable, and well-researched person. If you take this approach, you will never be unpleasantly surprised. If you enter expecting less than the best and you happen to get the best, you'll be at a disadvantage. On the other hand, if you enter expecting the best and get less than the best, you'll have the advantage.

▶ Directed interview

Basically there are three types of interview styles. **The directed interview is one used by most personnel department interviewers for screening.** It follows a definite pattern. The interviewer works from an outline and asks specific questions within a certain time frame. The interviewer has a checklist and makes notations about the candidate's responses. Most professional interviewers use the directed interview. It is of the least value because it is too structured and impersonal to get at the personality of the candidate.

▶ Nondirective interview

The second type is the nondirective interview. It is generally used by nonprofessionals and has a loosely structured format, one where the interviewee is allowed to talk about that which he wishes. The questions are broad and general, and they invite the interviewee to take control. The interviewer acts more like a moderator than anything else. It is an excellent format for bringing out an interviewee's personality. Since most non-professional interviewers go into interviews with no formal preparation, they are not set up to conduct a directed interview so they try and get the interviewee to talk. The result is a semi-nondirective interview.

▶ Stress interview

The third style is the stress interview. For the interviewer this can be a lot of fun. For the interviewee who is unsophisticated, it can be sheer hell. The stress interview was developed by the Germans prior to World War II. Initially, and in its classic form, it consisted of taking a close-up film of a candidate's face while he was being administered painful electric shocks. This crude technique has been refined over the years, and now it generally consists of long periods of silence, challenging your opinions, seeming to be unfriendly or brusque, and other attitudes directed toward making you uncomfortable.

It is extremely infrequent that a selection interview is entirely a stress interview. The most effective interview is a combination of the nondirective and the stress types. At the hands of a skillful interviewer, you can be led through a maze of ups and downs, and an amazingly accurate picture of your personality will emerge within thirty minutes.

Most interviews contain a certain amount of stress by their very nature. The introduction of intentional stress will be something that you will notice if you are alert. For example, if you are answering questions and suddenly the interviewer, and let's assume she's a woman, lapses into silence and stares at you, she's introducing stress into the interview to see how you'll react. If you fidget or start tapping your fingers or look down at your shoes, your actions tell her something—and it's not good from your point of view. If, on the other hand, you return her stare pleasantly and expectantly without showing signs of agitation, you've probably passed the test.

Variations on the theme of stress interviews are the group and board interviews.

▶ Group interview

The group interview is used where there are many interviewees and either one or several interviewers. It was devised to select officer candidates for the armed forces. Normal one-on-one interviews with résumés and reference checks had not been reliable in determining natural leadership ability. In this method, a group of candidates was assembled and assigned a task to accomplish as a group. The group was then observed during its performance.

It is said that a group will always stratify and that eventually a leader will emerge. Weinland and Gross in their book *Personnel Interviewing* say that "this person is apt to be what is called a 'natural leader.' Since he has no credentials, he must win the acceptance of the group and cannot be put in place merely by an external influence."

In a group interview, none of the normal rules hold. You should have a big advantage over other interviewees because the purpose of the group interview is not explained. In a business context, it may be presented as a group discussion. Since you know that the purpose is not to study what is said or the opinions expressed but to determine some characteristics of how you interact with the other members of the group, you should try to determine the characteristics for which interviewers are searching and direct your attention toward the group.

The group interview is rarely used in the United States, but it is a method of which you should be aware in the unlikely event you are faced with it.

▶ Board interview

Another type of stress interview is the board interview. This is one in which there is one interviewee and many interviewers. A typical board interview is the defense a doctoral candidate must make of his dissertation, commonly called an "oral examination." The federal government sometimes uses the board interview. It is perhaps most common in industry in interviewing for higher-level corporate positions, such as president or vice-president.

How you should handle yourself in a board interview does not differ greatly from the normal interview. The only added factor is that there is more than one person, so you cannot concentrate on establishing a rapport with one person. **If you're uneasy, the best way to handle it is to pretend that you are talking to only one person, the one who is questioning you.** In this way you may forget the other eyes that are upon you, and you may, in your mind's eye, convince yourself that you are in a simple one-on-one interview. The two important rules are to be relaxed and to maintain your confidence.

▶ California State Assembly fellowship stress interviews

An excellent example of the group and board interviews is conducted by the California State Assembly in awarding fellowships for their ten-month program. Charlotte Ashmun, who has been both an interviewee applying for a fellowship and, subsequently, an interviewer evaluating candidates for fellowships the following year, gives a unique description of the process:

It is a four tiered interviewing system. The first three stages have to do with getting the fellowship itself and the final stage has to do with the placement once you are a Fellow.

First you fill out an application form and there are usually about five hundred applicants for eight fellowships. That's used to screen.

The next stage is a Board Interview that consists of a committee of about nine academic people from throughout the state and Assembly staff who interview you alone. They ask political questions and theoretical questions and quite a range of questions as to how you would deal with problems.

Then the final stage is a Group Interview with the last group of finalists. You go through a process which involves three rooms full of interviewers. The interviewees are divided into three groups also. You go into each of the three rooms in succession and have a discussion on a policy topic.

There's no interference by the interviewers. The entire process is done by the interviewees and their intergroup reactions and that sort of thing.

It's terribly effective, but it's pretty frightening, too.

They're looking for how articulate you are, how well you think over a policy issue and they're also looking for how well you deal with other people. In a legislative setting, that's very important. They're not looking for people who are going to be abrasive. They're not looking for people who are going to be all talk and no content.

I wasn't impressed with the validity of the test when I went through it. But the next year I participated in it and saw the comparison of the notes by the interviewers and their discussion in choosing who should be selected for the program and who should not. Then I saw that as I stayed with one group all day long and followed them through their process, it became clear quickly who would make it as a Fellow and who would not.

Some people were too shy and would not speak up about their thoughts. In the position that the fellowship holds with the Legislature you're in front of committees and are asked questions about the bills you write by the committee members with the press there and you can't be so shy and retiring that you can't support the bill that you've been working on.

Additionally, a staff member has to be able to stay a staff member and not to try to be too much of a star. So although it was good to be able to give some guidance to the group and keep them on the track, if you were trying to make yourself look good to the disadvantage of everyone else, that was viewed quite negatively.

 ## Know what the interviewer is looking for

Each interviewer, no matter what type of technique she uses, is trying to fill a specific position. She will have formulated a set of specifications for that position, and there will be certain characteristics she will be looking for.

When the group interview was devised by the armed forces during World War II, it was used to determine the leadership characteristics of the candidates. The interviewers were looking for the person who could take charge of the group naturally. If you knew the purpose, you could gear your performance to that objective.

Directly contrary to this goal is the group interview conducted by the California State Assembly. Even though the same format is used—the group interview—the assembly is looking for opposite characteristics: people who will **not** exert their leadership characteristics, people who can function in a staff, advisory role and leave the leadership to the assembly-man for whom they will be working.

Once again preparation emerges as of great importance in determining how to approach an interview. If you know what the interviewer is looking for, you will have a tremendous advantage over the other interviewees because you will be able to key your performance to those characteristics. This knowledge alone may not land you a job offer, but it can protect you against making a gaffe that might result in rejection.

▶ How to handle stress

The cardinal rule to remember whenever stress is introduced into an interview by an interviewer is to retain your composure. No matter what you're feeling, try to exhibit calm. If you recognize the situation for what it is, you can just say to yourself, "Aha, this is a stress situation and he's trying to see if I'll get flustered." But the interviewee who hasn't heard of stress techniques and isn't prepared will be taken by surprise. If he's unsure of himself to begin with (and most interviewees are), stress will bring this uncertainty to the fore rapidly. Be aware of stress and be expecting it. When it comes, you'll pass with flying colors.

I have discussed interviewing with a great many interviewers over the years. Almost without exception the only ones who have read any books on the subject are people in the personnel field, who do only prescreening interviews. Those who make the actual selection, the managers and supervisors, have little knowledge of the science of interviewing. They conduct their interviews without reference to whether to use a directed or a nondirective interview or whether to apply stress. They simply proceed on intuition. They care not what their style is called. They will talk to you in the manner they feel is best geared for them to make their primary determination, which is whether they like you, whether they develop a good feeling about you.

CHECKLIST

★ An interview is a confrontation between two people when the understood purpose of the confrontation is for at least one of the two to make an evaluation of the other.

★ Always expect to meet a conscientious, knowledgeable, and well-researched person.

★ A directed interview is structured, impersonal, and generally used only by screening interviewers.

★ A nondirective interview is one where the interviewee is allowed to talk about that which he wishes.

★ A stress interview is designed to make the interviewee uncomfortable and to bring out his insecurities.

★ Most selection interviews are a combination of the nondirective and stress types.

★ A group interview has many interviewees and either one or several interviewers.

★ A board interview uses several interviewers.

★ Try to determine before the interview what the interviewers will be looking for.

★ Be aware of stress. If you are expecting it and recognize it when it is introduced, you will be better able to handle it well by retaining your composure.

4

THE SCREENING INTERVIEW

There are two basic manners in which you may be interviewed for a job. The first is to meet with a member of the personnel department for a screening interview. The second is to be interviewed by the supervisor or manager to whom the open position reports. In large organizations the latter follows the former. Probably more often than not, there will be no screening interview.

The screening interviewer, and let's assume she's a woman, has generally been trained in interview methodology. She follows the rules and formats in which she has been trained and probably will have digested most of the theories set forth in books on how to interview.

The selection interviewer, on the other hand, is generally not so trained and exposed. He will probably be unaware of methodology, types of interviews, stress, formats, and other techniques. This is the far more common type of interview. Secretaries are interviewed by potential bosses, clerks by the chief clerk, laborers by supervisors, and so forth. Only in a very structured organization can you expect to be faced with a screening interview. This chapter deals with how to conduct oneself with a "trained" screening interviewer; the rest of the book deals with the generally "untrained" selection interviewer.

▶ **Motivation of the screening interviewer**

☞ Her motivation is very simple. She does not want to send an obviously unqualified candidate to the supervisor who is requesting an employee. Therefore she is looking for a solid background. She will ask questions relating to work experience. She will probe for areas of inconsistency in your résumé. She will try to find out if you have lied on your résumé or in what you have told her. What kind of personality you have will be of little importance to her.

Sharyn Cole, director of placement for the giant Los Angeles Bonaventure Hotel, says, "The screening interview is a process of elimination. You try to weed out unacceptable candidates."

John Munro Fraser, in the third edition of *The Handbook of Employment Interviewing*, sets forth the view of the personnel function in conducting an interview:

We must get at the facts of a candidate's previous history; and we must go into it as thoroughly and in as great detail as is possible in the time available. . . . it is upon facts alone that a sound assessment can be established.

☞ *Even though the purpose of a good selection interview is not to get facts (which may be derived from résumés and ref-*

erence checks), facts are precisely the purpose of the screening interview. Since your purpose is to get past the screener to the selection interview, when you recognize a screening interview, you may put it to your benefit by providing the interviewer with the facts she so fervently desires.

It's to your advantage to help the interviewer feel that she has accomplished her purpose. Since the purposes of screening and selection interviews are different, it is important for you to be aware of who is conducting the interview. If it's a screener, you approach it one way because you know that she is looking for facts.

If, on the other hand, you are being interviewed by a supervisor to whom the position reports, you are faced with an entirely different situation. Whereas the screener has been trained in how to conduct an interview, the supervisor probably has not. He will probably be looking for personality traits and be making intuitive judgments about you.

More important, the supervisor has totally different motivations from the screener, who need worry only about being criticized by the department head making the requisition. While she does not want to be subject to such criticism, the final hire decision is not hers, so she can fall back on the excuse that her job was only to weed out obviously unacceptable candidates.

But the supervisor who makes a mistake and hires someone he later has to fire has cost the company thousands of dollars. A new employee naturally has to orient himself before he becomes totally productive. During this orientation period he is being paid his wages. Since he is very much less than completely productive during this period, the company is not getting its money's worth in work product. But it is making an investment in the future.

When the supervisor recognizes his mistake and lets the person go, the future is no longer a factor. That investment has gone down the drain. It has been estimated that a bad hiring decision on a top manager costs $30,000, a middle manager $15,000, and a lower middle manager $3,500. That's what companies figure it costs them to train someone. Not only is that money gone forever, but the time lost is an additional expense to the company because the hiring procedure must begin anew.

So the supervisor isn't just worried about being criticized by his boss for making a mistake. He has very real financial and organizational pressures with which he must deal.

▶ Screening interviewer wants facts

Each selection interviewer is different; each makes decisions based upon his prejudices.

☞ Despite all the pressures that are placed on selection interviewers to make a good decision, the way they arrive at their judgment is not scientific. You must recognize that no matter what they say they are looking for, they are going to reach their conclusion based upon the feeling they have after the interview about the interviewee. The way you think, the way you express yourself, what you say, how you say it, your manner and style, all are more important to the selection interviewer than the bare facts on your résumé. It is a very **personal** assessment.

In the screening interview, there is very little personal involvement on the part of the screener, who will probably never see the candidate again after the interview. She needn't worry about how the candidate will get along with other people, because she will not have to work with him. Further, she will not be subject to criticism on the point of personality because it's not part of what she's looking for. Her motivation is a relatively negative one: not to make a mistake in evaluating the facts for which she can be criticized. For example, if she sent a candidate for executive secretary to an executive and it was discovered that the candidate didn't know how to type, the screener would catch hell. If it was found that although the candidate typed 100 words per minute, but had a terrible personality and alienated the executive, the screener would not be subject to criticism at all. Her responsibility is not to make personality assessments but to analyze the factual data and determine whether the candidate has the skills and experience to qualify for the position. Therefore she is very careful that her judgments are backed up by cold, hard facts. Since she does not have the power to make the hire decision, her intuitive feeling about the candidate is irrelevant.

▶ How a screening interview works

The screening interviewer will take a clinical approach. She will work either from a written outline of points to cover or from an outline she has developed over the years. She will take notes and make notations when she discovers a point she wishes to document. Although screening interviewers are taught to try to establish a rapport, the fact remains that their approach is coldly impersonal.

A typical approach is suggested in *Personnel Interviewing*, a 1952 book that proclaims it was written "to fill the long-standing need for a thorough treatment of the aims and techniques of business interviewing in our modern industrial society." The authors, James Weinland and Margaret Gross, give four basic principles of interviewing: "1. The interviewee must be dealt with as a person. 2. The interviewee must be oriented. 3. The interviewer must maintain good communications. 4. The interviewer must be just." They amplify by stating that "modern management has recognized the fallacy of [the] thinking . . . [that] personnel to be used were thought of as so many units of work."

A supervisor interviewing to fill a position that reports to him would be unlikely to view a candidate the same way he would a machine or a typewriter because he knows that he and his people will have to interface with the person hired.

Many screeners do not view the candidate as a person. To them he is nothing more than a unit to be shuffled to another department head for further evaluation. Thus the interview is, by definition, impersonal.

Weinland and Gross continue in their guide to the personnel interview with such explanatory segments as "What a person is." If you comprehend that the screener has been trained by reading books that tell her what a person is, you may understand the attitude of the screener and should be better able to prepare for her.

Most books on personnel interviewing are read by only those who conduct screening interviews. But although they are directed toward supervisors as well as personnel people, the supervisor who has read even one book of this sort is as rare as a sailboat in the Sahara. A supervisor's job is not to interview but to perform a certain function (such as manufacturing a widget or selling that widget or keeping the books of the company). So when he does job-related reading, the books he reads deal with manufacturing processes or the techniques of selling or how to make debits and credits. As important as interviewing technique may be to the portion of his job that pertains to hiring and managing people, he doesn't think about how to interview until he is faced with the situation. When that occurs, he simply conducts it using his intuition.

The screening interviewer, on the other hand, has but one function—to conduct interviews—so she will probably confine all her job-related reading to the art and science of interviewing. She may know very little about the job for which the candidate is interviewing or about the supervisor to whom the candidate will report if hired. She works in a vacuum. She receives a requisition for a position with bare outline requirements. What does she do? She matches facts with facts. The purpose of this interview is simply to verify facts on the résumé and to endeavor to elicit more facts.

☞ Uppermost in the screener's mind is not to find the best person for the position, not to make a judgment on the candidate's personality, not to determine the candidate's thought processes; it is to ensure that the person interviewed has the qualifications in terms of education and experience for the position.

What is written here is not intended to be critical of the screening function. The job is a difficult one. But you must recognize that a screener is just that, a screener. The function a screener performs is valuable because it saves the supervisor precious time in interviewing and rejecting obviously unqualified candidates.

If you survive the screening interview, it is generally an indication that your qualifications for the position are acceptable as far as the facts are concerned: you have enough experience and there is nothing on your résumé or in your background to disqualify you (such as a record of convictions of crime or unexplained terminations from prior employment).

The screening interview is mostly a clerical function, consisting of checking the facts on the résumé, probing factual areas that may not be mentioned on the résumé, and filling in gaps in time that may appear on the résumé.

A serious personality conflict that emerges during a screening interview could result in rejection at this stage, but it is something that would occur only if you brought about the problem, since the interviewer is not probing in this area.

Knowing this going into the interview, you should conduct yourself accordingly. You should give the interviewer the facts for which she is searching. You should be pleasant and avoid controversy. Above all, avoid volunteering facts for which the interviewer is **not** searching.

The screening interviewer is an expert at her job, which is to discover a reason to reject you and not send you on to the next stage, the selection interview. She does not have the power to hire you, but she does have the power to reject you. And she will reject you for any reason that makes her feel that you are not qualified and that she would be subject to criticism for not rejecting you.

If you're bland, she'll probably pass you on and you'll reach the next stage, which is the most important because you'll be meeting the person who can offer you a job. But if you volunteer something for which she was not searching, it cannot add to your position. It *can* detract if it strikes her wrong.

Since you have nothing to gain, don't put yourself in the position of doing something from which you can only maintain the status quo or lose.

Therefore, in the screening interview, the key is to follow the interviewer's lead. In this case alone, it is best not to try to exert any control of the interview. She'll ask what she wants to know. Leave it at that. Once you find yourself in the same room with the person who is going to make the hire-no hire decision on you, you must assume responsibility for the content of the interview. Hopefully you have done your research and you know something about him, the company, and the position he is trying to fill.

Above all, recognize that you are breaking into his routine. His normal day does not include a selection interview. He's got all the responsibilities of his job on his mind, in addition to trying to find an acceptable employee. Therefore, he is probably completely unprepared for the interview, and he's wondering what he's going to do to make a determination to fill this vacancy, how he's going to do it, and how he can do it in as short a time period as possible.

This book deals with the selection interview conducted by the supervisor to whom the successful candidate will report. The screening interview is mentioned here because it is an interview that qualifies a candidate for the selection interview. It must be recognized for what it is.

CHECKLIST

★ A screening interviewer is looking just for the facts.

★ A screening interviewer is looking for a reason to reject you rather than a reason to accept you.

★ The purpose of the screening interview is to weed out unacceptable candidates.

★ A screening interviewer is well trained in the art of interviewing; a selection interviewer is not.

★ Don't volunteer anything in a screening interview.

★ Let the screener control both the flow and the content of the interview.

★ Avoid controversy.

5

ENTHUSIASM

"Nothing great has ever been done without enthusiasm," said Emerson. Enthusiasm is important for both the impression it leaves on the interviewer and for the effect it has on your outlook.

Paul Ivey, in his book, *Successful Salesmanship*, defines enthusiasm as "a spirit which animates the whole body [face, voice, and actions] and makes an attractive and convincing salesman out of an assortment of dead flesh and bones." I'd go a bit further. **Enthusiasm is the exhibition of fervent interest.**

When you take part in an interview, it is not enough to be interested or to say you are interested. You must show that you are interested through your actions.

I've conducted so many interviews where well-qualified interviewees sat and answered questions as if they were going through some sort of initiation rite. When the interview is over, they just leave. Whether this methodology of being interviewed is because of a misconception that it is wise to play "hard to get" or simply a lack of knowing how to act, their demeanor comes across to the interviewer negatively.

▶ Display an interest in the interview

The interview is an event in itself—something different from an offer or a job—and you must display an interest in it.

You don't have to prostrate yourself in front of your interviewer, and let's assume he's a man, begging for a job about which you know nothing in order to be enthusiastic about an interview. I've had many interviews in which I found out early that the interviewee was not appropriate for the job, but I was so interested in finding out more about him that my enthusiasm was unbounded.

Once I interviewed a law student who was interested in working only where he could use his proficiency in the Mandarin dialect of the Chinese language. It was obvious to both of us that the interview would not result in a job offer for him. But he was so enthusiastic about his training in Chinese and his work in Panmunjom, Korea, that it resulted in one of the longest interviews I've ever had. He was enthusiastic about telling me about his interests, and I was enthusiastic to learn more about him. As a result, even though the goal each of us sought, a job offer, was not achieved, this interview stands out as one of the most memorable ones I've ever had, and it was solely because of his enthusiasm. I have recommended him to a couple of corporations that had international departments, and I still keep him in mind years later.

 You can be enthusiastic about yourself, your interests, the interviewer, or his company. The point to remember is that without enthusiasm, you'll risk coming across as a dud.

◗ Categories of selling yourself

A large part of an interview is you as the interviewee selling yourself to the interviewer. Therefore it's well to know the techniques of selling.

The basic goal of an interview for selection is to determine personality traits. In *Successful Salesmanship*, Paul Ivey breaks the personality of a good salesman into four categories. The first is **enthusiasm.**

◗ Sincerity

The second is **sincerity**, which goes hand in hand with enthusiasm. If you generate a phony enthusiasm for something, such as a job about which you know nothing, two judgments may be made, both of them negative.

First, the interviewer may conclude that you're so hard up for a job that you'll take anything and reject you on that basis. Or he may conclude that your enthusiasm is insincere, which indicates a trait of dishonesty. Dishonesty, whether it is gleaned through lying or insincerity, can be grounds for immediate termination of consideration.

For this reason you should generate your enthusiasm for something in which you are genuinely interested.

◗ Tact

Ivey's third facet of personality is **tact.** Most good interviewers will bring up a controversial subject or interject stress into an interview by saying something with which he knows you'll disagree. How you handle this situation is a main test of the interview.

To disagree with tact, your response must first agree, then disagree. For example, you may say, "Yes, I see what you mean, but . . . " or "That's a good point. On the other hand . . . " If the agreement does not precede the disagreement, your answer will not have been tactful.

▶ Courtesy

The fourth aspect of Ivey's analysis of personality traits required of a good salesman is **courtesy.**

A lack of courtesy will probably be disastrous to the interview. You can be discourteous to the interviewer in many ways: in the way you dress, in the way you speak, in the way you ask questions, in the way you stand and sit, in the way you shake hands. If you arrive late for an interview dressed in a slovenly or unkempt manner, you are showing a lack of courtesy. If you slouch or are inattentive, your lack of courtesy will be noted. The use of profanity or telling of obscene jokes may be received as a lack of courtesy.

Courtesy is consideration of the feelings of others. Unfortunately society today seems to be moving in the direction where a lack of courtesy is the norm. "Doing your own thing" implies a disregard of one's obligations to others. The truly courteous person thinks of how his actions will affect others before he acts. Displaying a lack of this consideration will not result in "admiration" for your "independence." Rather, it may result in your leaving the impression of being a boor and could terminate any chance you might have had for further consideration.

▶ A word on validation

One of the problems with books that purport to tell you how to act is the problem of validation. Many people will read what I say in this book and either forget it or won't believe it. They won't apply it to themselves. They'll read it and then just let it drift away as summer drifts into fall, slowly, unnoticed, until one day it's forgotten completely.

☞ In order to make this book—or any other book you read—work for you, you must apply its principles while they are fresh in your mind. The methods I relate in this book work. The examples I give actually occurred. If you apply them to your own situation they can help you.

Years ago I read Dale Carnegie's *How to Win Friends and Influence People.* In it he tells how to get people to like you. One of the methods he suggests is to get them to talk about themselves. He tells of picking out some small thing you notice about someone and asking about it. He gives examples, as I do here, of the way this has worked for him and others in the past.

I read all this with a somewhat jaundiced eye, assuming that the examples were there just to fit the rule he was laying down. I didn't think much about it until one day I was sitting in a barber's chair. I had never visited this shop before so I didn't know the barber. Worse, he was extremely taciturn. So I sat in an uncomfortable silence as he cut my hair, responding to my few attempts at conversation with grumbles.

Then I remembered Dale Carnegie. I tried to discover something about him and his shop upon which I could comment to see if Carnegie's method could really work. Finally he lathered my neck and, after stropping his straight razor, he started shaving my neck. I commented, "Gee, that sure is a sharp razor."

That simple comment was akin to "open sesame." He told me that his father had given him that razor, that it had come from Germany, and that he had used it for years. "There's not another razor like this in America," he said. He was as proud of that razor as a parent of a child. He talked and talked and talked about his razor. I was interested, not only because his story of the razor was unique, but because my innocent remark had opened a mirror to the man's heart.

No longer withdrawn, he was warm and friendly. I was excited because I had never dreamed that the rules that I had read in Carnegie's book would work so well. I stayed after he had finished my haircut and talked with him for fifteen minutes while he worked on the next man. When I left, he said he hoped I'd come back because he "really enjoyed talking to me," even though all I had done was to ask a question or two while he monopolized the conversation.

One of the best ways to project enthusiasm is to try to make the other person enthusiastic.

I had turned a silently morose barber into a William Jennings Bryan of fire and brimstone just by asking him about his razor. This was the love of his life, apparently, and he was enthusiastic about it. His enthusiasm was contagious. It made me enthusiastic just to listen to him. Although I had little interest in his razor, his tremendous emotion conveyed itself to me and I was interested in his enthusiasm.

My barber story is not the exception that proves a converse rule. I am constantly amazed at how often it works to bring people out of themselves. When I was practicing law in London, I used the Middle Temple law library to do my research. The American section was on the top floor, and there was rarely anyone else in there but me and the librarian, a wizened old fellow who never opened his mouth or acknowledged my presence.

One day, after months of coming and going, I noticed him reading a book on gardening. Although I know little about flowers, I was raised in a house that had a large garden, and one of our flowers was hibiscus. I stopped by his desk and asked if there were hibiscus in London. He opened like a blooming flower, told me of his garden in Cornwall, the flowers in it and the years he had devoted to it. From that point on we were bosom buddies.

When you've successfully brought someone out of themselves in this way, you'll be amazed at the rewarding feeling you'll have. I doubt if there's anything I'd rather talk about less than gardening, but I was never bored by the librarian's discussions. The combination of his enthusiasm and the success of my ploy worked to keep my interest peaked.

It's not enough simply to ask a question. You have to project genuine interest. And if you get a response like I did from the barber and librarian, you're going to be interested. It won't matter if he's talking about the time and methods he uses to observe grass growing; if he's turned on about the subject, you're going to be spellbound, if not by the subject, certainly by the emotion you have sparked.

The most an author can do is to offer his advice and ideas. It is up to the reader to decide whether to accept the advice and then to decide whether to use it. You may read this book, find it entertaining, and even believe it. But if you don't try the things outlined here, it will be to no avail.

I urge you to lose your inhibitions and give the techniques a whirl. I'm sure you will find that you'll get far more out of an interview, are less nervous going in and more confident during the interview. You should find that your interviews will flow more easily and that you will establish a better rapport with your interviewer. Best of all, whether you get a job offer or not, you'll come out of each interview feeling that you have learned something new. Each interview is different because each interviewer is different.

▶ Treat the interview as an experience

Each interview will probably present you with a different challenge. It's exciting to go into an interview knowing that you'll be presented with the challenge of interpreting the interviewer's personality. Maybe you'll need to discover his interests. Maybe you'll need to talk about yourself and your own interests to find a common ground. Even though you can expect similar things from each interview, the challenge is that each interview is unknown from the point of the personality of the interviewer. If you view it this way, you will retain your enthusiasm for each interview.

▶ Attitude

The enthusiasm that you project is directly affected by your attitude. If your attitude is bad, there's no way that you can be enthusiastic. Having a bad attitude is not limited to a negative outlook. There's more to attitude than thinking, "Boy, I don't have a chance in this interview."

I conducted an interview at a law school several years ago that epitomizes how a bad attitude can affect an interviewee's enthusiasm. The interviewee showed up dressed as if he were going to play football in the mud. He wore a dirty sweatshirt with holes in it, dirty blue jeans, and old Adidas sneakers. Although he had an excellent scholastic record, he responded to my questions sullenly and abrasively. Finally, after the videotaping was over, I asked him if he showed up for all his interviews dressed that way.

This was what he was waiting for. All the rancor exploded. "If they don't like the way I look, the hell with 'em!"

This fellow was so proud of his anti-establishment posture that it dominated his personality. His antagonism for the way people dressed permeated the interview. Lighted bamboo shoots stuck under his fingernails couldn't have affected his interview worse.

His goal in the interview was to make the point that he would do, say, and dress as he pleased and no one was going to change him. He knew in advance that his dress was atypical for an interview and that it would be noticed. He waited during the entire interview for me to bring it up, and when he got his chance, he exploded.

He sat through the entire interview waiting for a fight. He flaunted his sloppy attire like a flung gauntlet. The content of the interview was merely prelude for his making his point. Even had the subject not been raised, he would have blown the interview because he came across as sullen and negative.

You radiate what you feel. If you enter the interview with a chip on your shoulder, you'll be written off in a trice. Your state of mind is terribly important to the success of your interview.

More often, however, the problem with attitude is not a childish temperament but a defeatist outlook. If you have been through a few interviews and have not received any offers or encouragement, it's very easy to become downcast and feel that you're a chronic failure. No matter how many rejections you may receive, you must keep your outlook bright and positive.

▶ Be willing to take a chance

You can develop methods to control your mind so that you enter the interview with a positive and enthusiastic frame of mind. A sense of failure or doom may not make much difference in a simple social contact, but in an interview it can easily cause you to fail. An interviewer is trying to get at the person beneath the surface. The worst thing that you can display is a sense of gloom or defeat. If you recognize that "no" is not always meant by the person who says it, initial rejections or setbacks will not diminish your enthusiasm.

George Bernard Shaw, in *Mrs. Warren's Profession*, said, "The people who get on in this world are the people who get up and look for the circumstances they want, and, if they can't find them, make them." When I was in law school, it seemed that 90 percent of my class was interested in practicing international law. Came the day when one of the largest international law firms on Wall Street visited campus to interview, the line to sign up was almost unending.

The interviewer was the senior partner in the firm. He also taught a seminar on international law at the law school. He interviewed for three days but made only one offer and that to one of the top students in the class. I was in the seminar he taught, along with another member of the class who had interviewed but been rejected and whose grades caused him to languish in the middle of the class. This student was determined he was going to work for that firm and so he was always well prepared for the seminar. Unfortunately the seminar was conducted by associates in the firm, not the partner.

Nevertheless, my classmate continued to prepare while the rest of us took it easy, knowing that our grade did not depend on performance in the seminar. One day the associate who was scheduled to appear could not make it, and the senior partner had to conduct the seminar—but he wasn't prepared at all. He was saved by my classmate, who virtually took over the class that evening. He was the only one who was prepared, and he talked for almost the entire two hours. The senior partner was so impressed that he offered the student a job and, in storybook fashion, the student is now a partner in the firm.

He showed enthusiasm and ingenuity to persevere for a job by impressing the one who had to make the decision. The job was offered not so much because of the interviewee's quality but because of the extra effort it took to figure out how to get the job after initial rejection. It's this way of thinking that will impress an interviewer time and again. Do something unusual to set you apart from the others. Be enthusiastic.

As a teenager, Eddie Rickenbacker wanted desperately to work for the Frayer Miller automobile manufacturers, so he started hanging around the plant on his days off. Finally Lee

Frayer noticed him and asked him why he was always hanging around every Sunday.

Rickenbacker told him that he wanted a job. Frayer said that they didn't have anything he could do. But Rickenbacker had noticed how dirty the place was and told Frayer that there was something he could do and he'd be back the next Sunday.

He arrived at 7 A.M. "with broom and brush" and worked feverishly. When Frayer arrived at 8:30, half the work area was spotless and the other half filthy. Frayer smiled and said that Rickenbacker had his job.

There are times when you can convince the interviewer that you are the person for the job. Not everyone is an Eddie Rickenbacker. He would not take no for an answer, but was willing to work with no promise of pay and no commitment. This ploy worked for him, and it opened up vistas of which an uneducated teenager in 1910 dared not dream. From that job he became a racing driver of world renown before World War I and, of course, finally president of Eastern Airlines.

Without the enthusiasm and the fervent interest in landing the job, these ploys wouldn't have worked because they wouldn't have been tried. Those of us in the seminar just weren't as enthusiastic about trying to impress the senior partner to prepare week after week on the off chance that we'd get the opportunity to show what we could do. One student wanted the job so badly that he was willing to put in the time and take the risk that it would all be wasted. He got his chance, and it will mean millions of dollars to him over his lifetime.

The Rickenbacker story is similar. He was so enthusiastic about working for Lee Frayer that he gave up a free Sunday morning to clean up a factory with no promise of remuneration. As a result of this gamble, he got a job that led him to his careers. It's conceivable that had he not had the enthusiasm to give up his Sunday to clean out the factory as a volunteer, none of the rest of his accomplishments would have happened.

 For you to take gambles, you must be so enthusiastic about the potential rewards that you are willing to risk what prospectively looks like certain failure. Without enthusiasm, your frame of mind will tell you that your actions are illogical and a waste of time. With enthusiasm your frame of mind is such that you will not admit of failure, and you will proceed with abandon.

CHECKLIST

★ You must **show** that you are interested.

★ Communicate your interest to the interviewer.

★ Be interested in the interview as an event in itself.

★ The four categories of selling yourself are
　　enthusiasm
　　sincerity
　　tact
　　courtesy

★ Lose your inhibitions and try what you've learned.

★ Enthusiasm begins with a positive attitude.

★ Think that you're going to win.

★ Make an impression on the one who is to make the decision.

★ Be willing to risk gambles on what may logically appear to be certain failure.

6

THE QUESTION AND
THE ANSWER

Essential to an effective interview is the ability to answer questions. No matter how many questions you may ask of the interviewer, and let's assume that he's a man, no matter how much control you assert, the essence of the interview remains locked into the format of questions asked by the interviewer. Whether your interview is successful depends on your ability to answer the interviewer's questions effectively.

You can be prepared for the type of question to expect by doing research on the interviewer, the company, and the type of position for which you are interviewing. But no interview is so completely structured that you can plan it completely in advance.

▶ The interviewer's feeling about you

The most important aspect that an interviewer gains out of an interview is a subjective feeling. *He is trying to find out what kind of person you are, and the questions he asks are the tools he uses to get at the inner person. He will develop a feeling about you from the interview, which will be more important than any notes he takes.*

Your goal, then, is to enhance this feeling. Because you are locked into the format of the interview, you must use the format to establish the proper rapport with the interviewer. It is the manner in which you answer the interviewer's questions that determines the success of the interview.

The questions and answers of an interview are merely the tools used to make an evaluation, the trees in the forest of impression. Your relaxation, your confidence in yourself and your manner are far more important than the words you use in your answers.

▶ Listen to the question

The first mistake that many interviewees make is that they don't listen to the question. If the interviewer is probing for certain facts, answer the question specifically. If the question is a general one, then take the question and turn it into what you want.

One of the causes of answers that do not address the question is that interviewees tend to make assumptions and then base their answers on these assumptions without stating them.

In their book, *Pairing,* George Bach and Ronald Deutsch warn never to "assume that you know what your partner is thinking until you have checked out the assumption in plain language; nor assume or predict how he will react, what he will accept or reject." This is easy to say but very difficult to do, particularly in an interview. You can't state your assumptions prior to answering a question as if you were writing a legal brief. Just as every question implies an assumption, every answer infers an assumption. People are not machines, and they don't converse like machines.

While psychological self-help books like *Pairing* treat things on a plane where all solutions are ideal and people react consistently, in reality this is not true. Each person is different from another, and each reacts differently. So while the scenarios that are acted out in these books always work out the way the authors intend, their successful conclusions bear little correlation to real life.

▶ The ambiguous question

☞ *In order to avoid misunderstandings or answers that avoid the point of the question, listen very carefully to the question and the way it is phrased. If it can be interpreted in more than one way, and you are unsure about the point, ask for a clarification.*

For example, one question that is often asked in interviews is "What are your goals?" This is ambiguous; people generally have several types of goals—personal, recreational, professional. When I ask this question, I am after two things. In addition to the content of the reply, I listen to determine how the interviewee, and let's assume she's a woman, will handle the inherent ambiguity. Will she say, "Well, I want to be happy and raise a nice family," or will the answer be, "I want to be the manager of the department," or "I've always wanted to break ninety on the golf course." How the interviewee interprets the question, the assumption she makes, tells me something as valuable about her as the actual content of the answer.

But very often the answer will be a request for a clarification. "What do you mean? Do you want to know what my professional goals are or what I want out of life?" There is nothing wrong with this answer. It is quite good. I then choose what I want to hear, and the interviewee answers accordingly. This type of answer takes no risk. There is a question in the interviewee's mind and rather than make the decision herself based upon an unstated assumption, she clarifies the ambiguity and then answers based upon the clarification by the interviewer.

In the situation of an ambiguous question, the ball is in your court. You can do with it what you want. If there's something you know you want to bring out during the interview and an ambiguous question is asked that gives you the opportunity to say what you want, don't ask for the clarification. Interpret the question the way you wish and answer it to your best advantage. If, on the other hand, the ambiguity troubles you and it does not give you a waited-for opportunity, ask for the clarification.

▶ The thinking pause

Another technique you may use in answering questions is to think over an answer before you give it, a method that can work to your favor. Yet often interviewees, intimidated by the power of the interviewer, are overly conscious of the time they are taking and tend to rush into their answers.

Asking for a clarification gives you time to think about your answer while the interviewer is clearing up the ambiguity. Many times a few seconds for thought will be a godsend; asking for a clarification is a good ploy to gain this thinking time.

An additional way to get thinking time is to use a bridge such as, "Let me see . . ." or, "That's a good question . . ." preceding your answer.

Time is not something to be considered in the context of giving careful thought before answering a difficult question. The interviewer is talking to you because he is interested. He has budgeted time to talk with you, so the few seconds you spend formulating your thoughts will not only not be resented; they will probably be noted with approval.

An example of an interviewee who was not intimidated by an interviewer who literally had the weight of the world on his shoulders is shown in the story of Dwight D. Eisenhower's initial interview with General George C. Marshall when Marshall was looking for someone to head up the Philippines and

Far Eastern section of the War Plans Division of the Department of the Army.

When Germany invaded Poland in 1939 and World War II was finally unavoidable, Eisenhower was a lieutenant colonel and felt that even with the war and America's almost inevitable involvement, he had little prospects for advancement. Despite this feeling, two years later, on December 12, 1941, less than a week after the Japanese had bombed Pearl Harbor, Eisenhower had been promoted to brigadier general and was summoned to Washington by General Marshall, the chief of staff.

Eisenhower and Marshall had talked only twice before, once in 1930 and once in 1939. Marshall greeted Eisenhower perfunctorily and then outlined the stark situation that was facing the United States in the Pacific: the devastation of the Pacific fleet at Pearl, the invasion of the Philippines, the lack of any effective air strength, the damage that was being wreaked by the Japanese army and air force, the critical supply shortage, the Japanese blockade. He painted a very dim picture of the situation. After he had set the facts before Eisenhower, he looked Eisenhower in the eye and asked, "What should be our general line of action?"

Eisenhower was taken aback. He had just stepped off the plane and had no real personal knowledge of the situation. Here was the man who had to make the decision, a man who had been well briefed and was on top of the situation, asking his opinion! Eisenhower was intuitive enough to recognize the importance of the question both for the war effort and for him personally. He said later, "His tone implied that I had been given the problem as a check to an answer he had already reached."

If ever an interviewee could have been pressured into giving an immediate answer, Eisenhower in that position at that moment in history was the man. Here was the newly appointed chief of staff asking his opinion of the situation in the Philippines where Eisenhower had served for four years. Yet Eisenhower kept his composure and did not reply off the top of his head. He asked General Marshall for a few hours to consider his answer.

Eisenhower returned later that afternoon with his recommendation: even though the situation was almost hopeless from a military point of view, he felt that the United States should do everything possible in their defense. Marshall replied, "I agree with you. Do your best to save them."

Marshall's assessment of Eisenhower was undoubtedly based as much upon the method of Eisenhower's way of answering the question as it was on the content of his answer. He wanted a man of judgment and depth, a man upon whom he could rely to make decisions based upon analysis and cogitation. The fact that Eisenhower displayed the confidence in himself to ask for time to formulate a reply must have impressed the chief.

This does not mean that you can ask for several hours before answering difficult questions in an interview. But it does illustrate the point that a few seconds of thoughtful silence before responding will not only not be considered a negative, it could be exactly what the interviewer is looking for.

▶ Where to look

Where do you look during an interview? Should you always look the interviewer straight in the eye and stare him down? Should you look away? This is one of the real traumas many interviewees go through during an interview. Of course, the best advice is simply to act naturally. Talk with the interviewer as though you were having a cup of coffee with a friend.

Dr. Gerhard Nielson of Copenhagen conducted a study of how and where interviewees normally looked, and you should be aware of the results. He filmed interviews on a fast-running camera. In replaying the films in slow motion, his results showed that there is actually very little eye contact maintained during an interview. The most an interviewee looked at his interviewer was 73 percent of the time, which means that he **didn't** look at him 27 percent of the time. One man looked away for 92 percent of the time. Nielson found that half of the interviewees looked away for 50 percent of the time.

Nielson discovered other interesting things. When people are speaking, they tend to look away; when they are listening, they tend to maintain eye contact. It's normal for you not to look at the person to whom you are speaking. But I have found that interviewees worry about this and feel they should always look their interviewer in the eye. Yet, as Dr. Nielson's study found, this is abnormal. Being abnormal, it would strike the interviewer wrong and could very easily make him uncomfortable.

Nielson also discovered that interviewees tend to look away from the interviewer when they start to speak. There is a subtle timing in speaking, listening, looking, and looking away. Interviewees tend to look away just before or just after the beginning of one quarter of their statements. Fifty percent of the interviewees look at the interviewer as they finish speaking.

Don't worry about looking the interviewer in the eye. If you force it, it will come across unnaturally and leave a bad impression. Try to treat the interview as a conversation and act as you would in such a situation. Remember that it's rare for an interviewee to look an interviewer in the eye all the time. If he did, it would be disconcerting to the interviewer. The best rule is to act naturally and not worry about eye contact.

▶ Eye signals

You should be aware of signals people make, often subconsciously, with their eyes.Even though neither party to a conversation may recognize the signals overtly, they may accept them as a nonverbal form of communication and act accordingly. You should be aware of these signals both as an interpretation for you to make of your interviewer and as signals you may be giving your interviewer.

Julius Fast, who has analyzed these signals in *Body Language*, explains that if you look away while you speak, it means that you're explaining yourself and shouldn't be interrupted. If you then look the other person in the eye, you are passing a signal to interrupt when you pause. But a pause without looking in the eye would mean that you aren't finished yet.

If you as a listener look away from a speaker, you are telling him that you are dissatisfied with what he is saying or that you are trying to conceal your reaction to the speaker's words.

To look away while you are speaking may mean you are uncertain of what you're saying.

If you as a listener look at a speaker, it is a signal of agreement; and if you as a speaker look at a listener, it's a signal of confidence in what you say.

These are some assumptions that people may draw from your actions during conversation. Your actions may thus easily result in their developing negative or positive impressions without knowing exactly why they come away feeling the way they do.

Never forget that the important thing that an interviewer derives from an interview is that intuitive feeling he gets from you. It's either positive or it's negative. More often than not he will not be able to specify the exact reasons for his feeling, but he will have developed them nonetheless. It may be derived from how you have handled silence or how you've answered one question or how you've acted during the conversation. Whatever it is, it's your task to enhance this feeling. It is therefore important to be aware of the signals you make during conversation and the typical reaction of others to these signals.

You can also use this information to make judgments on your interviewer. You can make assumptions based on where, when, and how he looks when speaking and listening.

Eye signals are something of which you should be aware but I don't think they are especially important. What is important is that you act naturally and that what you do with your eyes is comfortable.

Psychologists tend to go overboard with their analyses of people's actions. As you can see from Fast's analysis, some of his assumptions from the same actions are inconsistent. It's easy to say that looking away while you are speaking means you are uncertain of yourself. But as Dr. Nielson's study shows, it is normal for a person to look away while speaking.

The premise that if someone is uncertain of what he is saying, he will look away while saying it is probably accurate. But to conclude that all people who look away while speaking are uncertain of what they are saying is absurd. Most people look away while speaking, and it's unrealistic to think that they are all doing so because of uncertainty. They look away because that's the way most people naturally speak!

I mention Fast's ideas here simply because they add to your awareness of what's going on in an interview. If you're worried about whether you should concentrate on your eye signals or just forget them and act naturally, it's much better not to think about where you're looking and let your eyes fall where they may.

► Treat every question as important

Interviews are generally short. Therefore you must be sensitive enough to recognize that each question has significance and that you shouldn't answer offhandedly, thinking that the interviewer is just trying to make conversation.

Act as if every question the interviewer asks has a purpose. If the interviewer is inexperienced, he may well be just trying to make conversation and keep things moving. But you can't rely on this judgment. If you assume he knows what he's doing and has a purpose for his questions, you won't be harmed if he doesn't. If you make the contrary assumption, you can be devastated. The purpose of the question may not be so transparent as the question suggests. A smart interviewer can determine many things from one response to one question.

Whenever you're tempted to throw away an answer, remember a story J. Paul Getty told about a test he once gave. He was concerned about the cost consciousness at one of his companies, and decided to test the attitude of his three top executives. He instructed the payroll clerk to make a five dollar reduction in each of the executives' next paychecks, and told the clerk to send any who complained to Getty's office. Within an hour of distribution of the checks, all three executives were in Getty's office, complaining that their checks were short five dollars.

Getty pounced on them. He told them that there were so many inefficiencies in the company's operations that the company was losing tens of thousands of dollars. The executives were blind to these inefficiencies, but when their paychecks had an inefficiency that cost them five dollars, they were on it like a rabbit on a carrot. Getty reports that this test cost one of the executives his job. What seemed to be a simple thing to the executives was actually a career-testing confrontation.

Seemingly innocuous questions can have great bearing on the judgment an interviewer may make on you. One interviewee told me of a lesson he had learned by not being attuned to the fact that every remark or question an interviewer makes may be meaningful. He was being interviewed for a position as a trainee by the buyer to whom he would report for a major toy manufacturing company. As a part of their selection process, he was required to take an IQ test. The interviewee had an IQ in excess of 150, and he scored the highest ever achieved on the test.

When he began the interview, the interviewer asked if the interviewee had been interviewing many companies. The interviewee replied that he had been looking for a job for about a month. The interviewer offhandedly said, "I guess you're getting tired of these tests, eh?" to which the interviewee smiled and nodded.

The interview didn't last much longer and, thinking over why, the interviewee realized that he had been tricked into admitting that he really didn't have a high IQ, that he did well just because he had been taking the same test over and over. In fact it was the first IQ test he had taken since he had graduated from college. He had made a noncommittal response to the buyer's friendly intimation merely to be agreeable. His failure to be alert to provide accurate information to each question or probe had cost him.

His response should have been along the following lines. "No, this is the first such test I have taken since I was a sophomore in college and I was somewhat surprised to find that you would require an IQ test for this position. Do you find that it adequately tests for an aptitude for being a buyer?"

This response not only gets across the fact that the test score was an accurate measure of IQ, but it puts the interviewer in the difficult position of defending the use of the test to a person who had scored very highly on it. If he does defend the accuracy of the test, how can he logically reject an applicant who had scored so well unless he finds some other reason as the interview progresses?

◗ The blockbuster question

Sometimes an interview will start with a real blockbuster of a question. The one that I think is the most difficult by far is, 'Tell me about yourself." You think that looks easy and innocuous? Have it sprung on you sometime at the beginning of an interview for a job you desperately want and then see if you think it's so simple.

What do you say? Do you tell him what's on the résumé? Do you tell about your love life? Talk about your outside interests?

If you've done your preparation, you know something about the interviewer, the company, and the job. You know what you want to say in the interview. Try to formulate an answer to this question **before** you go into the interview so that you can jump right into it. It is actually a terrific opportunity to take charge of the interview and talk about your strengths.

You can talk about what you've done of which you're most proud. You can talk of your qualifications and why you think you want the job and why you think you would do a good job. You can say anything you want.

A question of this sort also tells you that the interviewer is probably fairly sophisticated. This question takes the control of the interview away from him at the outset, so you know that he's sitting there making judgments on you right away, not only from the content of your answer but from **how** you choose to answer.

▶ Questions about your private life

Sometimes interviewers will ask insensitive questions about your private life, probing not only areas about marriage, but also lovers and so on. This commonly happens in interviews for real estate sales positions where the rationale of the interviewer is that he wants to be sure that, if offered a position, you will devote sufficient time to selling real estate.

I don't think it's ever appropriate to answer questions of this sort. Questions like, "Do you have a boy (girl) friend? Do you spend weekends together?" are nobody's business but yours. They have no relation to your job, and nobody has a right to butt into your personal affairs. The only reason that interviewers ask this type of question is that interviewees are generally so docile that they will answer them, mainly because the format of an interview is not unlike a lie-detector test. The interviewee feels that if she does not answer a question, she'll blow her chance for an offer.

Balderdash. When a question like that is asked, you should have the courage to answer honestly but without rancor: "I'm applying for this position because I feel it's something I want to do. If I were not planning on devoting sufficient time to performing the duties required, I wouldn't be taking your time, and mine, to apply and go through the interview process. What I do in my private life and with my free time will have no effect on how I perform the functions of this position."

If he asks a question like this or any other offensive question, he will know he is skating on thin ice, so he will accept a gentle rebuff. But you can't be so sensitive that you have a whole list of things that you won't answer. If it's a major point and your objection is legitimate and applicable to a group as a whole, it's perfectly acceptable to decline to answer. But if you do it too often, you have either had the misfortune of being interviewed by Attila the Hun, or you're too sensitive and will encounter great difficulties in getting beyond the first interview.

In any event, don't let the interviewer intimidate you and *push you around. Your private life is private and is of no legitimate concern to him.*

▶ Skeletons in your closet

Virtually everyone has some skeleton in the closet of which she is ashamed or embarrassed. If yours is job or school related, there is a fairly good chance that the interviewer will strike upon it. You should prepare your response very carefully on this point because an unexpected thrust at a vulnerable area can be devastating.

Let's take an example. Assume that you left one of your previous jobs because you had a fight with your supervisor. Assume further that you had worked there for a considerable period of time, so you can't omit the job from your résumé. It's possible that an interviewer will ask you why you left. You must be able to respond to this question honestly but in a way that places you in a favorable light.

You should review the circumstances of the situation and come up with a truthful explanation that cannot be contradicted by a reference check. On your side is the fact that previous employers are reluctant to give out derogatory information on former employees, so the facts of the situation may be difficult for your interviewer to discover from any other source. It is helpful, however, for you to know what kind of a reference you will be given. You may have a friend make a bogus check on you with the prior employer to discover how a real reference check will be handled. Then you can face an interviewer knowing with a fair degree of confidence how an inquiry by him will be received and tailor your response accordingly.

It is not a bad answer to say that you had a personality conflict with your supervisor and were unable to work it out so you felt that it was better for both you and the company if you left. That's all right to use to explain one departure on your record. But if you use it more than once, the interviewer may decide that you are a difficult person to get along with—and this can be the kiss of death. Just about everyone has had one or two people with whom they have had personality conflicts and have been unable to get along. But if you've had this unfortunate circumstance with a supervisor more than once, you will be at a disadvantage if the subject comes up in an interview. As a result, you had better have another honest, verifiable reason for leaving more than one job. This is where preparation is most important. Your answer must be honest. If this is your skeleton, you must be prepared for it. It may not arise, but if it does and you haven't planned it well in advance, the likelihood of your surviving the question is slim.

☞ Of course you may have other skeletons. If there's something that you hope you won't be asked, you should know exactly what you're going to say if he **does** ask you about that. This is another area where your demeanor in answering the question is almost as important as the words you use. If it appears to the interviewer that you're equivocating or lack confidence in your response, it won't matter much what you say. The impression you will have left will probably lead him to conclude that a negative inference is justified. So know what you're going to respond and respond with confidence and candor.

Admitting a weakness is disarming. You could say, "You know, he just had the type of personality that made it very difficult for me to get along with. I like to be able to admire and respect the people I work for, but there was something about him that I felt was wrong. I handled the situation very poorly because my attitude seemed to be communicated to him and it alienated him, so he treated me in a manner that I felt to be unacceptable. I blame myself for this entirely and have felt badly about it. Since I recognized that he rubbed me the wrong way, I probably should have been able to work out our differences in some manner that would have been agreeable to both of us. But it was a very difficult situation for me. I was so close to the situation, so emotionally involved, that I was unable to take an objective view of it and it just seemed to get worse. Looking back, I can see some things that I probably should have done to alleviate the situation, but the best that I can say now is that I learned from the experience and if it ever arose again, I think I'd be better capable of handling it."

Answering a question in that way will show that you accept full responsibility for the situation. Even if you don't feel responsible for the problem, this type of answer will place you in the best light and will protect you against a bad reference check. Basically you're saying, "This guy was a jerk, but I should have been able to handle that. Therefore it's my fault and I'll know how to deal with it if there's a next time."

If, on the other hand, you tell the interviewer, "The guy was an absolute loser. No one could get along with him. I had finally had him up to here and told him to shove it," and he checks and gets a similar response about you, he will probably reason, "If the supervisor is so bad, why is he still working there?" The conclusion he'll reach is that you've put him in the middle of a bad disagreement and have asked him to make the choice of whom to believe. Why should he make any kind of choice? He'll just say that it's not worth the risk of getting a potentially disagreeable person into his organization and reject you.

Don't keep fighting the battle. If you accept responsibility and say that you learned from the experience, you disarm any negative things that may be said about you and project an image of peacemaker rather than warrior.

▶ Grievances against former employers

Don't talk against a former employer. The advice your mother gave you, "if you can't say something nice about someone, don't say anything" applies here. Even if you have a legitimate grievance against someone, don't talk about it. If you are asked, just say something that will dissuade further questions. You can turn the interviewer away from the subject with a tactful answer like, "I don't feel it's fair to them for me to discuss our disagreements with other people." This will not only turn away any further inquiries; the interviewer should consider you a person of discretion.

I had an interview with a potential client once who had a great deal of lucrative legal work that she needed to be done. We discussed the details of the work and then I asked her about her prior attorney. This loosed a wave of virulence about the lawyer. She castigated him for every indiscretion of which she could think: he overcharged; he did poor and sloppy work; he was never available to talk with her; he continually pressed her to pay his exorbitant fees. Her diatribe went on for fifteen minutes.

The impression she made upon me was completely different from that which she had intended. My conclusion was that no matter how much work she had for me, she would feel that she owned me. She would call anytime, day or night. If I happened to be working on other problems, she wouldn't understand. Finally, she would eventually be sitting in some other lawyer's office talking of me as she was now talking of her last lawyer. I declined the client mainly on the strength of the feeling I developed during her criticism of her former attorney.

An interviewer can be expected to form the same sort of judgment when faced with intense criticism of a former employer by an interviewee.

There are two sides to every story. While you always feel that you are in the right and your antagonist is in the wrong, your antagonist feels the same way (that he is in the right and you are in the wrong). Therefore if the interviewer were to check your story with your antagonist, he'd get an equally forceful version that would picture you in a poor light. Once again, if you take this approach, you have not taken care of the interviewer. You have placed him in the middle, and he has very little incentive to take your side. Not that he will take the other side against you. He will probably conclude that hiring you isn't worth the risk and reject you. He doesn't want to have someone who will be sitting in another interviewer's office a year hence talking of him in the way you are talking of your antagonist to him. Without question, that is one of the things that will go through his mind while you are relating the dismal details of your battle.

If you refuse to discuss it, you enhance the feeling the interviewer will receive. Even if he checks out the situation with the third person and receives a negative report, it's probable that he will respect you for not talking against someone with whom you have a grievance, and the empathy thus gained may be enough to overcome any negative feelings your antagonist may have been able to arouse in the interviewer.

If you have an antagonist of this sort, and it is discovered in an interview, you are faced with the problem of defusing the situation. There are only two alternatives open to you. First, you can reveal the entire situation when asked. This will set the interviewer up as judge and jury, and all things being equal, will probably result in a rejection.

Second, you can tactfully decline to discuss it. This has the advantage of trying not to involve the interviewer and can work to your advantage.

Of course if the interviewer presses you, you have no choice but to give your side of the story. In this event you won't have the problem of involving the interviewer. You will have tried to take care of him. You will have gotten across the point that you are discreet. But if he continues to ask for specifics, a refusal on your part to discuss it could leave the impression that you have something to hide. This, buttressed by a negative report from your antagonist, would probably be enough to cause a rejection.

So if the interviewer refuses to allow you to drop the subject, you will have to give your side of the story. You should then feel free to relate it, but in as dispassionate a manner as possible.

Some interviewers will probe points such as this for reasons entirely unrelated to what you may be thinking. They probably have little interest in the facts of the situation or who was right or wrong. What they may be examining is your ability to maintain control in an emotional situation.

If you relate the circumstances and become emotional while telling the story, it could indicate to the interviewer that you do not have sufficient control over your emotions, and this could result in a negative inference. Although you want to present your case in a forceful enough manner to counterbalance your antagonist's story, you want to do it as unemotionally as you can.

▶ Answer specific questions specifically

☞ *You should always direct your reply to the interviewer's query. If he asks for specific information, don't play semantic games with him. If you don't wish to give it to him for some reason, it's better to decline frankly than to beat around the bush by giving him an evasive answer.*

▶ The throwaway joke

Over the years the many interviews I have conducted tend to run together in my mind, but naturally a few stand out for one reason or another. One fellow I interviewed for a position with a client gave me a classic answer when I asked him what he felt his biggest asset was. "I had my wife interview me last night," he said. "That was one of the questions she asked and we discussed how to answer it. I guess my biggest asset is that I'm always on time."

I was nonplussed. Here was an entree for him to tell of his most glowing achievement. He could have picked anything from when he won his high school debating medal to his courage on the battlefield to his industriousness, morality, candor, likeability. Anything. Instead he used this opportunity to crack a joke.

His revelation that he had gone through a mock interview was a calculated risk. Naturally it's better to try to appear spontaneous, but to admit that you've prepared as much as this is not necessarily a negative. It shows the interviewer that you care enough to do some homework, and that's all to the good. Another point in his favor was that he was perceptive enough to anticipate a question that generally takes interviewees by surprise. Up to this point, his admission that he had gone through a mock interview with his wife and had anticipated this very difficult question was working in his favor.

When an interviewer assesses someone for a job, he makes many subtle judgments. But his visceral reaction is probably the most important.

The judgment I made is typical of how fast a little thing can blow an opportunity. After telling me of his mock interview, he was ahead of the game. He had showed me that he had the interest to prepare and that he cared.

But then he answered the question: "I guess that my best asset is that I'm always on time." If someone has enough interest to go through a mock interview, if he has the perception to anticipate one of the toughest questions, I expect a good, well-reasoned answer.

His answer indicated one of two things to me. First, the easy judgment is to accept the answer at face value. His biggest asset is that he's on time. If that's the case, I don't want him. I want someone who has more to offer than that.

The second judgment is that he's making a joke. But this judgment leads to another: here is a man undergoing an interview that could change his life. He is asked a serious question, one that begs for an intelligent response. He's asked a question that is obviously meaningful to his interviewer. Yet his response is a flip joke. This judgment leads to rejection faster than the first. A response like this indicates a shallow, insensitive individual with whom I would never entrust serious problems.

Another thing I considered was his apparent lack of depth. Had he thought how such a response would be received? Isn't it possible that a flip response to a serious and penetrating question would be insulting to the interviewer?

I did not offer this man a job. I did interview him again to ensure that my initial judgment was correct. To enforce my opinion, I brought along someone who would be working closely with whomever I hired. I took him to lunch, where he launched into a monologue that lasted an hour and fifteen minutes. My first impression was confirmed: the man had an abrasive personality and was insensitive. Even so, I checked the references he gave me. Both people were surprised that they had been given as references and, under probing questioning, revealed their dissatisfaction with his personality and his ability to get along with others.

Here was a man who had three opportunities and flunked all three. Had he answered the question he had anticipated more maturely, perhaps I never would have received the vibrations that I did. But then, that's the purpose of an interview and it is what separates the good interviewer from the bad and the good interviewee from the bad.

Joking is something that is very risky to try in an interview. The first time producer George Martin got the Beatles together for a recording session, they were unknown and very young. Martin, trying to make them feel comfortable, explained what was going to occur and told them if they didn't like anything to let him know. George Harrison replied, "Well, for a start, I don't like your tie." As funny as this is now that the Beatles are history, it was especially inappropriate at the time because the tie Martin wore was new and he was proud of it. Why risk offending someone who is going to make a decision on you for the sake of an ephemeral joke that won't gain you anything and may cost you his goodwill?

Harrison's choice of a joke is an example of the worst kind he could have picked, one that makes fun of another. He should have realized that poking fun at the dress of the man who was giving them an audition would be insulting and not inspire his sympathy.

☞ The lowest form of humor is that which picks on another. If you feel the need to joke, it is better to make yourself the butt of the joke so you will not run the risk of offending your interviewer. You may project a frivolous image and hurt yourself in that way, but you will not hurt yourself by insulting him.

Humor is not necessarily bad in an interview, but it must be used in an appropriate spot and in good taste. You must be mature enough not to use an opening for a serious answer as a straight line for a comedy routine.

▶ Dual purpose questions

Questions often have a purpose other than the one that appears from its content. For instance, the question, "What have you done of which you are most proud?" seems to ask for you to tell of some outstanding accomplishment. The question seeks to get you to tell of something you've done well, but there is more to it. Whenever you are asked in a vague and general way about your past accomplishments in this manner, the question also probes your ability to make a decision.

A question such as this is calculated to flood the mind with ☞ *recall of many accomplishments. An indecisive person may be unable to make up his mind about which achievement to discuss. If you choose one and talk of it, even though there may be many things you've done in the past of which you are proud, you will have shown that you are a person who can make up her mind.*

It's not the purpose of this chapter to tell you how to answer each question with which you may be confronted in an interview. In the appendix is a list of commonly asked questions. You should review these. If any of them gives you difficulties, work out an answer so if you're hit with it in an interview, you'll be ready. Remember the old saying: "To be forewarned is to be forearmed."

CHECKLIST

★ The most important aspect that an interviewer gets out of an interview is a subjective feeling about the interviewee.

★ You must enhance that feeling.

★ Listen to the question.

★ If the question is ambiguous, you should either interpret it in your way and say what puts you in the best light or ask for a clarification.

★ Use ploys to get thinking time: ask for a clarification or use a bridge.

★ Don't worry about thinking for a few seconds before you answer.

★ Don't worry about eye contact; just act naturally.

★ Assume that every question is asked for a purpose.

★ Be ready for the blockbuster question.

* Handle the offensive question firmly but tactfully.
* Tactfully decline to answer questions about your private life.
* Prepare good answers for questions that may probe skeletons in your closet.
* Find out how your references will respond to a check.
* Accept responsibility for personality conflicts.
* Don't put the interviewer in the middle of a battle.
* Don't talk against a former employer.
* If you must discuss a bad situation with a former employer, do so dispassionately.
* Answer specific questions specifically.
* Don't respond to a serious question with a flip joke.
* If you joke, don't make the interviewer the butt of it.
* Recognize dual purpose questions and answer them decisively.

7

ASSUMPTIONS

A few years ago when I was engaged in a negotiation with another lawyer, I instantly developed a negative attitude toward him because he wouldn't look me in the eye; he always seemed to be gazing at a spot just over my left shoulder. This grated on my nerves, and I took it for a sign of weakness and uncertainty on his part.

A few months later I was spending the weekend with a friend and her family in Old Greenwich, Conn. She had her college roommate over for dinner, and her roommate looked at me exactly as had the lawyer I considered weak and uncertain.

My reaction was similarly negative. As the evening progressed my friend brought up the fact that her roommate was wall-eyed, and it had caused her no end of self-consciousness.

I felt mortified and guilty. Clearly my judgment on the lawyer was wrong. He had the same problem, and I had assumed a conclusion without establishing the facts. By this injustice I had insensitively rejected him for a reason that didn't exist. In fact, it took great strength of character for him to persevere in a profession where eye contact is so important and, for him, virtually impossible.

It's difficult to judge things solely by using a factual basis without making assumptions. But it's essential that your reactions and actions in an interview are based upon facts to the largest extent possible. In addition to their inherent inequity, erroneous assumptions acted upon can be disastrous.

▶ When "yes" doesn't mean "I agree"

Don't delude yourself that the interviewer agrees with everything you're saying merely because he nods agreement. You can be easily led down the primrose path by your assumption that you've hit upon a common belief when in reality his reaction may not signify agreement at all.

Averell Harriman had an especially close relationship with President Franklin Roosevelt during World War II, and he commented on Roosevelt's penchant for using the word "yes" when he didn't really mean "I agree."

He agreed but in the manner which I have long since learned, cannot be accepted as a commitment. . . . Lack of understanding of what the President means when he nods or says "yes" has led to much bitterness on the part of . . . businessmen who assume they have the agreement of the President when all they have, really, is an indication that the President is not prepared to argue the point with them. . . . It means that he hears and understands what you are saying, but not necessarily that he agrees to it. Anyone who assumes otherwise is engaging in wishful thinking, or is not very astute."

 A nod of the head or a brief "yes" may mean just the opposite of agreement: it may be a signal that the interviewer has heard all he wishes to hear of that subject and wishes you to get on to something else.

▶ Unexpected reactions

When an interviewee shows up for an interview with me, dressed in a slovenly manner, I generally ask about it. One time the response I received was, "I want people to judge me for the kind of person I am, not for the clothes I wear. Do you think it mattered what Clarence Darrow wore?" He sat back smugly, thinking that he had scored a tremendous point. He had assumed that my immediate reaction would be to conjure Darrow's defending a great cause in his studiedly unkempt dress. Unfortunately he was wrong.

Reactions can be illogical. It is almost impossible to determine in advance how an interviewer is going to respond. An interviewee takes a particular risk when he assumes an aggressive position to someone whom he has known for less than ten minutes.

My reaction to his reference to Clarence Darrow was to think of Earl Rogers, a renowned trial lawyer of early twentieth-century Los Angeles, called by many the father of demonstrative evidence and the witness box dénouement so often seen in Perry Mason mysteries.

Darrow was indicted for bribery in the *Los Angeles Times* bombing case and Rogers, in a brilliant defense, got him acquitted. Rogers's trademark was to show up in court dressed in formal evening wear, and that's what I thought of when my smug interviewee mentioned Darrow. Irrelevant? Illogical? Perhaps. But an interviewee has no way of knowing how an interviewer will react to an assertion. This particular interviewee had probably never heard of Earl Rogers. But he took a great risk assuming that I shared his belief that Clarence Darrow was the Mahatma of the legal profession. Because his assumption was wrong, his thrust was not just impotent, and it created a negative feeling in me.

This epitomizes the great risk we all take in the interview process. The person conducting the interview is a stranger. We cannot hope to discover much about him—his education, intelligence, and prejudices. We are at sea in a world of uncertainty. For this reason, if for no other, we must base our actions on facts as we perceive them in the short period of time at our disposal. To venture into the unknown by making rhetorical parries is to step into an abyss. You may hit the bullseye and score grandly. On the other hand, the odds are much in favor of missing the mark and creating a negative feeling that no amount of rehabilitation can overcome.

▶ Observe the interviewer

☞ *The facts upon which you must base your assumptions must be gleaned from your reading of your interviewer. You should pay very close attention to him and be sensitive to his reaction to you.*

The importance of being sensitive to the differences found in interviewers is illustrated by the reactions of two men, both presidents of corporations, to the way interviewees answer questions. Dr. Robert Langford, president of Bertea Corporation, says, "I'm not looking for quick, fast responses. I'm looking for responses that are logical and make sense."

Poul Moller, president of USA Petroleum Corporation, has an entirely different reaction: "I interviewed a man I hired about two months ago. He really came across like a go-getter. Any question I asked he had a quick reply. He never had to hesitate. Some people have to hesitate on a question. He never hesitated. He knew the answer right away. That really impressed me."

What is a positive for one interviewer may be negative with another. For this reason you must pay close attention to the interviewer and how you are being received.

☞ Remember that you should never answer a question just to please the interviewer. You must come across as yourself, an honest person who knows himself and is comfortable that way. But you do have to have the discretion to observe the interviewer to see if you are offending him. There's a big difference between being honest and being stupid. Your honesty does not diminish if you back off from a subject or manner of acting if you observe that it is not being well received. Would you tell Beverly Sills how much you detested opera? Discretion does not imply dishonesty. Rather it is simple courtesy.

The perceptive person can detect hints others give that sub-consciously communicate their feelings toward him. Sharyn Cole of the Los Angeles Bonaventure Hotel says, "I don't consciously use body language myself. But if an interviewee knew what he was doing, I'm sure that it would work. If I sit up straight, it means that the interviewee is getting on my nerves, or I'm getting defensive. If I sit back it means I'm relaxed and that would be a good sign for the interviewee."

Each interviewer may be different, but they will all give off clues as to how you are being received. You should be perceptive enough to observe these clues and adjust your interview accordingly.

If you notice what seems to be a negative response—the interviewer is sitting up straight, fidgeting, folding his arms, or looking away while you are talking—you should take the hint and either stop talking or change the subject. If you strongly feel that the body language of the interviewer is telling you that you are not being well received in what you're doing, don't compound the problem by continuing. When some people perceive they are not being well received, they become nervous and talk too much. If you have the perception to read the body language, use it to your advantage and stop doing whatever it might be that is causing the negative reactions.

▶ False conclusions

There are two types of assumptions interviewees invariably make that they shouldn't. The first is to project an assumption about the interviewer and answer questions based upon this assumption, as discussed earlier. The second is to walk out of an interview and say, "Boy, did I do lousy there! I'm sure I made a bad impression and blew my chance." How do you know how the interviewer reacted to you? You really don't know what he was looking for. You may have connected on all cylinders, yet you're projecting your standards upon him and making the assumption that you failed.

Dr. Robert H. Schuller, in his book *Move Ahead with Possibility Thinking*, relates a classic story about a Chinese man who had one horse and one son that points out the errors of assuming. The horse ran away and the neighbors commiserated on his bad luck.

"'Why,' the old Chinese said, 'How do you know it's bad luck?'

"Sure enough, the next night the horse came back to his familiar corral . . . leading twelve wild stallions with him! . . . The neighbors heard the good news and came chattering to the farmer, 'Oh, you have thirteen horses! What good luck!'

"And the old Chinese answered, 'How do you know that's good luck?'"

A few days later his son broke his leg falling off one of the new horses and, once again the neighbors tried to console him on his bad luck.

"And the wise father answered again, 'How do you know it's bad luck?'

"Sure enough, a few days later a Chinese war lord came through town and conscripted every able-bodied young man, taking them off to war, never to return again. But the young man was saved because of his broken leg."

Don't make assumptions based upon your narrow frame of reference until all the facts are in. The man to whom Schuller referred was the epitome of the pragmatist: he made no judgments upon events. He accepted them and let the events move to their inevitable conclusions. To conclude that the things that happened were "good luck" or "bad luck" for him required him to make assumptions that he was unwilling to make. He acted and waited.

So too, after an interview, you should not make evaluative judgments because they will be based upon assumptions that will have no basis in fact. How can you know whether you had a "good" or a "bad" interview? How do you know whether you made a "good" or a "bad" impression?

☞ *You waste your time by making such judgments. You are in the worst possible position to evaluate your performance. In the first place, you certainly are not able to make an objective appraisal. Second, you don't know what the specifications for the position are. Third, you can't possibly put yourself inside the head of the interviewer to determine the feeling he got from you.*

Finally, what good will it do for you to make some kind of a judgment on how the interviewer thought you did? You can't go back and redo the interview. You can't change what's happened.

I once had an interview with a man for a position with a client of mine. I came away from the interview thinking that he was probably the worst interviewee I had seen in months. The next day the executive search agent who had set up the interview called for my response, and I told him that I wasn't interested in pursuing the matter further. He expressed great surprise, "When I talked with the applicant he was jubilant. He felt that he had come across well and that you had been very favorably impressed!" All that applicant did was to delude himself and build himself up for a great letdown. He had apparently made some very basic erroneous assumptions about me and my reaction, and had walked away from the interview thinking that he was very close to receiving a job offer.

All of us wonder about how we did in an interview for a position in which we are interested, but wondering serves no purpose. You waste your time and you can either build yourself up for a great letdown or you can worry yourself into a state of acute depression. Wait until you discover what the interviewer's judgment on you has been before you evaluate the interview. If he rejects you, then you can gain from reviewing the interview objectively to determine what happened so that you can better prepare for the interviews in the future. If he asks you to a follow-up interview or makes you an offer, you can then bask in the glow of an interview well conducted without the possibility of being cruelly let down by believing in a false assumption.

▶ Don't be intimidated by your competition

Inevitably, during the course of the interviewing process you will see other candidates and they will impress you. They will be good looking, well dressed, charming, and sophisticated, and you'll assume you don't have a chance. You will feel a failure immediately. You'll wonder, what's the use? This other person has it all wrapped up.

Don't assume yourself into a position where you are intimidated by style rather than essence. An interviewee is the poorest judge of how an interview went. When I was preparing my interview service, I videotaped interviews with three people as samples. One of the interviewees was an experienced, outgoing person who had style. Another was sort of average, and the third was a shy and retiring introvert.

In my own mind I rated them with the extrovert on top and the introvert capable of impressing no one. After I showed the interviews to prospective clients, I asked them to rate the interviewees. To my surprise, the introvert was rated first by more prospects than the extrovert. The reasons they gave included their assessment that they felt that his personality was more amenable to their type of operation. The extrovert came on too strongly for most of the people who saw the interviews, and they felt that he would be difficult to get along with.

Time and again an interviewee will tell me that he felt his interview was poor, only to have that person receive more offers than the seeming "superstars."

 Interviewers are rarely misled by style as a substitute for substance. They are looking for a personality that will fit in with their operation. A hail fellow, well-met may be a smash at a party, but as a candidate for a job he might not have the advantage that his sophistication may project.

▶ Think positively

Norman Vincent Peale says in *The Power of Positive Thinking* that if you expect the best, you'll get it. Of course that is not always the case, but the point that he makes is one that is valid as much in the converse as it is in concept: **If you think you're going to fail, you undoubtedly will.**

Two things that happened to me as a young lawyer point out the importance of attitude and expectations upon success. I had recently become counsel of a large division, and I was going to have to negotiate with a potential supplier. I had heard stories about the abilities of their attorney and how smart and vicious he was. I was intimidated. I went into the meeting assuming that he knew a lot more about the problem than I and was more experienced. I just hoped that I could come out of the negotiation without making too much of a show of my ignorance.

The negotiation was the disaster I had anticipated. The other attorney was arrogant and intimidating. When I'd say something, he'd laugh snidely as if to say, "How can anyone be so dumb?" Afterward I was in a blue funk. Here was my first chance to leave a good impression and I had blown it.

A few weeks later I had to fly east with another negotiating team. I was told that the people with whom I would be negotiating were very nice and easy to get along with. I had no fears.

It turned out that they were not "nice." In fact they were tougher and more knowledgeable than those in the first negotiation in which I had participated. But I went in confidently and unworried. I locked horns with them on several key points and emerged unscathed and victorious on each. The word got back to management that I was a tiger, and my reputation was made.

Later I met the lawyer who had so intimidated me in the first negotiation. By this time I had built confidence in myself and didn't make any assumptions about his superiority. It turned out that he was all show and no substance. When I didn't let him intimidate me and didn't assume failure, he caused me no problems.

Bad assumptions can so intimidate that you can be defeated before the fray begins. The only cure is to prepare as best you can and have the confidence that you can handle anything that arises. Don't compare yourself with other candidates because you don't know what the interviewer is looking for. Be yourself. It's just as likely that the interviewer is looking for you as it is that he's looking for someone completely different. If he is looking for someone completely different, you wouldn't be happy in the job in any event, so it's better to find that out.

▶ Don't key your performance to false assumptions

There are two distinct disadvantages to making assumptions not based on fact and trying to key yourself to those assumptions in your interview. The first is that you might be right in your assumption and play the role so well that you'll get the job. Then when you return to your normal self, you won't be happy with the job and the employer won't be happy with you. You'll be worse off than had you never gotten the job. The second disadvantage is that your assumption may be wrong, and they may have been looking for someone like you actually are and you'll role play yourself out of an opportunity.

There is, however, one assumption that the wise interviewee should make prior to any interview. Although most selection interviewers are not knowledgeable in the art of conducting an interview, **you should assume that the interview in which you are to participate is going to be professional and that the interviewer will be well prepared. If you assume the best and get the worst, you are not going to be hurt. But, if you assume something less than the best and get the best, you're going to be at a disadvantage.**

▶ Analysis of specific technique

One of the most sophisticated interviewing techniques is that used by the Life Sciences Division of Whittaker Corporation in performing their contract with the Saudi Arabian government to provide hospital and related services in Saudi Arabia. They must hire specialized individuals, such as doctors, nurses, technicians, and administrators who are of a high caliber.

The positions in Saudi Arabia have many negative factors, the primary one being a tremendous culture shock. Thus the selection process becomes a most important component of Whittaker's performance. Each hire costs the division approximately $10,000. Therefore, if someone is hired who does not fulfill the minimum contract time period of eighteen months in Saudi Arabia, the mistake is extremely costly to the company. Not only are they out the $10,000 it cost them to make a selection, they have lost a significant period of time and performance.

Jerry Kenefick is the manager of the international recruitment office of the division. His staff consists entirely of professionals in the fields for which they are interviewing. Doctors interview doctors, nurses interview nurses and so on.

They receive approximately sixty résumés a day from all over the United States. Ninety percent are from people who are obviously not qualified. The remaining 10 percent are pre-screened by telephone; this interview eliminates 95 percent of the remaining 10 percent. So out of the résumés received, 0.05 percent are invited in for the second stage interview.

Cheryl Vanos, the logistics coordinator, characterizes the interview as a "negative-stress" one—that is, the negative aspects of the position are stressed to weed out those who would not survive the tour of duty.

Kenefick says that although their interview process is designed to pick those who are not only qualified but will be able to adjust to the Saudi life-style, the final decision is based upon a feeling that he and the other interviewers have about the candidate. He can't define how he arrives at this feeling but states that it is generally accurate and that he and the other interviewers usually arrive at this feeling within the first ten minutes of the interview.

Kenefick's interview consists of two parts. Initially he is looking for qualifications, so he goes down the résumé with the interviewee item by item. If he discovers a gap or an inconsistency, he'll ask about it. Any intentional misrepresentation can seriously damage a candidate's chances.

The second phase is to determine if the interviewee is the right kind of person to go to Saudi Arabia. He asks many questions to get into the inner person: What do you do in your spare time? Do you have close friends? When was the last time you got together? What was the last movie you saw? He probes these areas because Saudi Arabian society is spartan by American standards. There are no movies, no churches, no television.

Interviewees generally try to give answers they feel the interviewer is looking for. A typical answer is, "I read, never watch TV, don't go to movies and like to be my myself." Kenefick will let this pass and then later in the interview (which may last from forty-five minutes to four hours, depending on the level of the position) will gently ask if the interviewee happened to see a certain television show or movie. Normally it turns out that the interviewee does like television or movies or American sports and has answered the way he did only to get the job.

Kenefick uses other ploys to get candidates to eliminate themselves. "Once," he said, "I had an interviewee who was dressed very fastidiously. Everything was perfect from his hair style to his shoe laces. As we talked, I dwelt on the size of the roaches over there, the fact that the flour moved constantly because of all the weevils, things like that. The interviewee actually had to excuse himself as I was talking because it upset him so. He came back and said that he didn't think he was interested."

If the candidate gets by Kenefick, he goes to the final stage by meeting with Vanos. Her ostensible job is to brief the candidate on life in Saudi Arabia.

"The interviewee has been through an entire day of interviewing with Jerry and the others," she says. "He gets to me and thinks that it's all over. So he tends to relax and drop his pretensions. He doesn't realize that I'm assessing him, too. He may confide his trepidations to me. Or he may inadvertently let me see what he's really like. After I'm through with him, I'll get together with Jerry if I have some doubts about him, and several times a candidate has been rejected because of my input. We have to be very sure that the person we hire will stick it out and perform in an acceptable manner once he gets over there.

"I remember one fellow whom we were interviewing as hospital administrator. He got to talking about his daughter and her fiancé. He exhibited a very low tolerance for her fiancé's goals and ideas. He came across as very inflexible. Well, how's he going to react when his forty-year-old head nurse comes to him and complains that she's been caught by the Saudi religious police for living with some American engineer and is going to be deported? She will be crying that she's forty years old, recently divorced and lonely, that she needs companionship. How's he going to deal with that if he doesn't have the tolerance to cope with his daughter's fiancé and his contrary ideas and life-style?"

Kenefick says that he probes candidates' motivation for wanting to go to Saudi Arabia. "Invariably," he says, "they say that they want to go for three reasons. One, they want to do good for Saudi Arabia. Two, they want to travel. Three, they have an adventurous spirit.

"My job is to get beyond these three reasons to the real reason. Are they running away from a divorce or an unhappy love affair? Why do they **really** want to go? Not that their reasons that they give initially aren't what they believe. They are generally highly motivated people and these are real reasons. But we know that there quite often is some other reason and if there is, we want to know what that is. Saudi Arabia is no place to recover from a broken heart."

Vanos wants "to hear that they are motivated by the money. Because in Saudi Arabia, when you have to be there for from eighteen months to two years, money is the thing that keeps you going in the final analysis. If they admit this, we can be more confident that their motivations are such that they will last for the term of their contract."

There are several lessons to be learned from this. First, always make the assumption that you are going to be exposed to a good, sophisticated interview technique on the part of the interviewer. Even though the chances are that the interviewer won't be as competent as Kenefick and his crew, if you prepare for the best, you'll be ready for anything.

Second, assume that every question is asked for a reason connected with the job, even if it sounds like idle chatter. The man who sharply criticized his daughter's fiancé didn't realize that this was being projected by the interviewer to an actual job situation and an assumption and judgment made thereon.

Third, don't assume that just because you're talking to someone other than the person who makes the final hiring decision, the interview is over. The interview lasts until you have accepted an offer or been finally rejected. Remember, there's many a slip 'twixt the tongue and the lip. Even though they make up their minds on you once, they can change at any stage.

CHECKLIST

★ A bold assertion you make can be met with an illogical reaction by the interviewer.

★ You can't discover an interviewer's quality and makeup in a short interview.

★ If you make a negative impression early with an assertion based on a false assumption, you will have a very difficult time reversing the impression.

★ Closely observe the interviewer and be sensitive to his reactions.

★ Observe the interviewer's body language and react accordingly.

★ If you perceive hints you aren't being well received, stop what you're doing that may be causing the negative reaction.

★ Don't make conclusions after the interview ends about how well or poorly you did.

★ Don't be intimidated by your competition.

★ Think positively.

★ Don't key your performance to false assumptions.

★ Assume that you are going to be exposed to a sophisticated, professional interview technique.

★ Assume every question is asked for a reason that is job connected.

★ Assume that everyone with whom you speak before an offer or rejection is made is making a judgment on you.

8

HONESTY

Honesty in an interview consists basically of three elements; truth, consistency, and candor.

There comes a time in every interview when you will be tempted to exaggerate your accomplishments. The interviewer may ask you how much money you're making, and you may decide to add a couple of thousand dollars a year to your actual earnings. Or he may ask you where you finished in your college class, and you may think there's little difference between the top third and the top quarter.

When you feel this temptation—and it strikes everyone, no matter how honest—remember this little rule: WHEN IN DOUBT, TELL THE TRUTH! Sir Walter Scott said it years ago in iambic tetrameter:
"Oh, what a tangled web we weave,
When first we practice to deceive!"

If you lie, and that's what an exaggeration is, it will haunt you for the rest of your days. A lie is a terrible cancer that, undiscovered, haunts the utterer with fear of discovery. Once discovered, it can destroy his credibility forever.

A person does not want someone working for him whom he cannot trust. If a prospective employee lies in the initial interview, the conclusion that an employer draws is that the prospect will continue to lie.

 Failure to tell the truth reveals a character trait that cannot be remedied. Once it is discovered that you have lied, things will never be the same again. It is something that cannot be forgotten. Human nature is such that the knowledge of a lie preys upon the subconscious. No matter how much we forgive, we do not forget.

The Thomas Brown affair

Perhaps the classic example of an applicant lying also epitomizes Hitler's "big lie" theory: if you're going to lie, lie on as grand a scale as possible because the bigger the lie, the more apt people are to believe it.

A young man to whom I shall refer as Thomas Brown (not his real name nor any of his aliases) applied to Harvard Law School and was admitted. His application listed a degree from Tulane University. Three years later Harvard discovered that this was false and forced Brown to withdraw from the university.

Two years later Brown was admitted to Harvard Law School again in 1973 under a different name. This time he claimed to be a graduate of Louisiana State University. He obtained loans of $2,500, the maximum amount a student may borrow.

Law school is a three-year program, and traditionally students spend the summer between their second and third years as clerks in law firms. Brown, who told the interviewing firms that his grades consisted of all A's, that he had been a football player at LSU, and that he had spent a year at Oxford, received offers from two of the largest law firms in Los Angeles, as well as invitations for follow-up interviews from major firms in other areas of the country.

Brown knew how to play his role. He wore a beard "to make him look older" (he was thirty-one at the time, claiming twenty-four), always dressed in a suit, drove a Mercedes, and dropped names judiciously. He gave the impression of wealth and would casually mention he was flying to Brazil one weekend, another far-off place the next.

He was undone while interviewing with a major New York firm. One of the partners had attended LSU and did not remember Brown's playing football. An inquiry caused his house of cards to tumble.

Brown was done in by the inevitable mistake that finds most lies. If there's a moral to the story other than remembering to tell the truth, it's that if you're going to lie, you might as well do it right. As long as you recognize that a lie found will disqualify you, it's foolish to waste it on puffing your salary by $2,000. Brown swung for the fences and almost made them. Had he finished interviewing after receiving the offers from Los Angeles and accepted one of them, it's conceivable that he'd be working as one of Los Angeles's respected lawyers. He didn't quit while he was ahead, so he lost.

Of course, I strongly recommend against any kind of intentional deception. Eventually one of the threads will break and they'll find out that you didn't play football at LSU or spend a year at Oxford or graduate from Tulane or get all A's. Then you will have invested years for naught, in addition to having your reputation ruined.

Brown ended up facing civil and criminal charges. As a tag-line to the tawdry story, Brown's wife was found to be a student in the Harvard Business School with credentials every bit as false as her husband's.

▶ You don't know how much the interviewer knows

Sometimes the interviewer knows more about you than you realize. A colleague of mine once recommended a friend to me for a position with a client for whom I was interviewing. He told me that his friend was dissatisfied where he was because he was making less than $20,000 per year and was looking for a higher paying position. I met with the friend and after an hour's amenable conversation I gently probed areas I felt important and casually asked how much money he was making. He told me that he was making "around $35,000." Of course, he had no way of knowing that his friend had revealed his salary to me. But that's the danger in lying. You never know the knowledge of the person to whom you are lying. Nor do you know the sources available to him to check out your stories.

Suddenly the tenor of the interview changed. Within the space of a few moments a metamorphosis occurred in him. The cocoon fell from this fellow and different colors shone through.

Whatever subject I broached was followed by a dogmatic diatribe defending his view, which was absolute. There was no moderation in his tone, no conversational amenity. He was a completely different person. For every topic upon which I touched, he had a position intolerant of any differing view I expressed.

☞ How much of this was an attitude that was there but that I didn't perceive and how much was caused by his lie, I can't say. But my opinion of him changed within five minutes. First was the unacceptability of his lie. I would not have made him an offer after the lie. Second, however, was the personality change. Did I see him with different eyes, or did **his** knowledge of his lie make him change?

▶ Fact versus opinion

☞ *There are ways to answer a question to your best advantage. Although nothing will end an interview faster than a perceived lie, you must distinguish between fact and opinion. If an interviewer asks how much money you are making, he is asking for a fact. There is no real way that you can hedge your answer without misrepresenting a fact, which is an almost unanimous choice by interviewers as the one thing that will definitely decide them against an interviewee.*

The two examples just discussed were misrepresentations of fact. But if the question calls for an opinion, you can shade your answer so that you show up to your best advantage without actually lying.

After I gave a lecture at a western university, a student came up to me with a real problem. He was ranked third in his law school class, but he had not yet received an offer, despite the fact that the recruiting season was almost over. He seemed to me to be eager, intelligent, and personable, so I asked him if he thought he knew the reason for his lack of success. He replied that he thought that his problem was that even though he had been invited to try out for the *Law Review*, he had declined and that the firms didn't like this. I asked him what reason he gave, and he said that he told them that he knew that the *Review* took a lot of time, and he didn't want to sacrifice his social life for all that work.

If I ever heard an answer calculated to turn off a prospective employer, that was it. I suggested in the future that when he was asked why he didn't try out for the *Review*, he tell them that he had observed how much time the people on the *Review* staff devoted to their work and how it caused them to neglect their course work. He was very interested in the courses he was taking this year, and he felt that it was more important for him to study them than to devote his time to the *Review* to the exclusion of his course work. He realized it was an honor to be invited to try out for the *Review*, but he felt he had to sacrifice that honor in the interests of ensuring that he could devote the time required to his courses. Although he recognized that not trying out for the *Review* could hurt him in interviewing, he felt that he would only have the opportunity to take these courses while he was in law school and, after long agonizing, had determined that it was better for him to forgo the prestige of the *Review* and concentrate on his studies.

This is not a misrepresentation of a specific, provable fact and therefore is not a lie that could be empirically disproved. The interviewer is asking for an opinion why he did not try out for the *Review*. When asked for such an opinion the interviewee should answer the question to his best advantage. The answer I suggested was a plausible, acceptable explanation that allowed him to get over a hump in his interview and resulted in the interviewers' evaluating him on the whole interview and not on one very bad answer that had a "halo" effect.

☞ Interviewers know that interviewees want to present themselves in the best possible light and will recognize that a certain amount of "puffing" will take place where an interviewee will expand his role in a situation to make it look as if he had more to do with the result than he actually did.

▶ Differing interpretations

Most occurrences are subject to different interpretations. **What must be distinguished is the intentional misrepresentation of an established fact from the embellishment of the interpretation of a situation.**

☞ In the former instance are examples of saying you made more money than you actually did, misrepresenting time periods in your résumé, saying you finished higher in your graduating class than you actually did. If you misrepresent a verifiable fact that is not subject to interpretation and it is discovered, you may terminate the interview process, or, if you have already been hired, you may find your job terminated.

People do not want someone working for them whom they cannot trust. A person who will tell a lie in an interview exhibits a character trait that is unacceptable to most people.

☞ Judgments made in the interviewing process are based on assumptions made by the interviewer drawn from information derived from the interviewee. If a person lies in an initial interview or on a résumé, it is reasonable to assume that the person will continue to lie on the job. What could be a worse way to start a relationship than to build it on the foundation of a lie?

▶ Consistency

☞ *Inconsistency is a trait that can be almost as devastating to your appearance of honesty as a lie. In order to be consistent, you have to know yourself.*

You must take great care to be consistent in your interviews, especially in a screening interview when you are faced with a person trained in conducting interviews that have as their purpose the revelation of facts.

One of the goals for which they strive is a reason to reject ☞ *you. They are looking for inconsistencies on your résumé and in what you say. If they get a glimmer of something wrong, they may ask the same question over and over in different ways to test what you have claimed. If you have told the truth, you generally have nothing to fear in an interrogation like this. But if you have misrepresented something, or if you have hedged an answer to show yourself in the best light, you must be very careful that each time you discuss that topic you say the same thing. If you once vary from what you said before, you may either be rejected for that or you may have to justify the variance.*

The selection interviewer, and let's assume she's a woman, is also looking for inconsistencies, but not with the same fervor that a screening interviewer may. The selection interviewer will probably not search for an inconsistency unless she gets a red flag to one of her questions. If you claim some accomplishment that she feels is beyond you, she may go into the subject in depth and probe the area to determine exactly what you did and how much you participated in the event.

For example, if I were interviewing the student who didn't try out for the *Review* and he told me that he wanted to devote all the time he could to his studies, I would let some time pass and then question him on his outside interests. If I then discovered that he played intramural sports, never missed a first-run movie, went to all the football and basketball games, and dated a different girl every night, I'd conclude that his reason for not trying out for the *Review* was inconsistent with his actions and would probably reject him on that basis.

▶ Candor

The third element of honesty is candor. As a rule, interviewees look upon a selection interview as a one-way street. On the one side sits the interviewer who is picking a person to fill an available position. On the other side is the interviewee who is applying for the position.

But it works both ways. The applicant is also an interviewer seeking to find if he is interested in the position. The selector acts as the interviewee to explain the position and "sell" the applicant that the job is right for him.

If something bothers you about a position for which you are interviewing, you should be candid about your doubt and express it to the interviewer. I counseled a man once who told me that he had turned down an attractive job offer because he had seen the interviewer, the vice-president to whom he would report, be abrasive to a subordinate. He said that he felt that he would not react well if he were treated in a similar manner. I asked if he had discussed the problem with the vice-president, and he replied that he had not. He had simply declined the offer. He felt badly about it because what he knew about the position stimulated him.

An interviewee or job applicant should realize that when a job is offered, it is a compliment. The employer is saying "I like you and I think you can do a good job. I am so confident of this that I'm willing to pay you to come and work for me." When a compliment is paid, it should be treated with respect. If for some reason the job offer is to be rejected, the interviewee owes it to both himself and to the offerer to state the reasons for the rejection. There are several reasons for this. First, it is courteous. Second, and more important as far as the interviewee is concerned, the offerer may wish to resolve the problems you have with the job by making it more palatable..

The person I was counseling had a fear that the vice-president would be difficult for him to work with. He made this judgment on the basis of one observed occurrence. He didn't give the man another chance. It's possible that his interviewer had just been released from the hospital or a close relative had died, or he had lost a lot of money in the stock market, or the subordinate could have been completely incompetent or he could have had some other disappointment about which the interviewee knew nothing. If he doesn't raise the point, he isn't getting the most out of his interview. He should try and get as much information as he can.

Had he turned down the position by saying, "I appreciate the offer, but frankly I am very much concerned about how you and I would work together. I consider myself a professional and, as a result, feel that I am due professional respect and courtesy. The way you spoke to Mr. Smith troubled me," he would give the interviewer an opportunity to face his main objection to the job and at least explain his actions.

Remember the advice previously given on assumptions. Don't base your decision on unqueried assumptions that may be erroneous. Be as certain as you can that your assumption is based on fact. You can do this by using candor and bringing your assumptions out into the open. If you think the job is an attractive one but you have grave doubts because of something about which you haven't spoken, bring it up and discuss it with the interviewer prior to making your decison.

One executive I knew made a terrible career mistake because he feared the use of candor during the interview process.

A reputable company had been trying to find a new vice-president of finance. It had been interviewing for over a year to fill a vacancy that had had several occupants the preceding two years. Obviously something was wrong.

He was contacted by an executive search firm, and the salary and fringe benefits were so attractive that he went on the interview, despite severe misgivings. He met the top management and was impressed. Still his doubts nagged.

He was made an offer that was beyond his wildest dreams: a large salary, a Continental, bonus, profit sharing, everything he had ever wanted. On the debit side was the fact that he knew that the three people in the job before him had only stayed a few months before leaving. He also knew that the company had had the vacancy for over a year. This troubled him, but he feared to bring it up.

Analyzing the situation later, he knew that his fear had two bases. First, he felt that a question about the turnover might offend the interviewers and cost him an offer. Second, he feared that what he might discover might cause him to have to reject an offer he knew he wanted. So he didn't broach the subject, took the job, and immediately found himself in the eye of a storm.

Apparently there were shenanigans with one of the recently acquired divisions that could subject the company to shareholders' derivative suits and the officers involved to extensive liability. Each of his predecessors had apparently discovered the problem quickly and resigned rather than become embroiled in such a dangerous situation.

My friend had burned his bridges, had large personal expenses, and couldn't afford to quit. His résumé had so many job changes that he felt he couldn't put his name out on the street, so he had to try to survive without participating in the problem and thereby becoming an accomplice.

He was stuck in a miserable situation for two years before an offer appeared at a much smaller company for much less money. He grabbed it without looking back.

Had he been candid and expressed his doubts, he could have discovered the problem prior to taking the job. Of course, the company wouldn't have admitted such a thing to a job candidate, but he could have listened to their explanation and then told them he wanted to talk to the previous men who had held the position. That most probably would have either terminated the company's consideration of him, or he would have discovered from his predecessors that the situation was sticky.

 It's never wise to accept or reject an offer if you have unexpressed doubts about something. Bring them out into the open. They may be unfounded, and you will be able to start your new position with a clear mind. Or they may have foundation, in which case you're better off knowing about it and not proceeding further (or proceeding further with actual knowledge of what you're getting into). In either case, you're much better off by being candid and expressing your doubts than keeping them to yourself.

CHECKLIST

★ Honesty consists of truth, consistency, and candor.
★ When in doubt, tell the truth.
★ An undiscovered lie will haunt you.
★ A discovered lie can destroy your credibility forever.

★ An employer does not want someone working for him whom he cannot trust.

★ Failure to tell the truth reveals a character trait that cannot be remedied.

★ Remember that you have no way of knowing how much the interviewer knows.

★ A lie can change your personality as your guilty knowledge of it affects your performance.

★ Distinguish between a question calling for fact and one calling for an opinion.

★ Always answer questions calling for your opinion to your best advantage.

★ Inconsistency can lead to an inference of a lack of honesty.

★ Be candid about your doubts and bring them up to the interviewer.

★ A job offer is a compliment, and you owe the interviewer the courtesy of being candid.

★ Don't base your decision on unqueried assumptions.

9

CONFIDENCE, NERVOUSNESS, AND RELAXATION

More often than not, confidence is what separates the successful from the failure. In *How to Pick up Girls,* author Eric Weber said, "It's the people who act most nonchalant and least uptight, most unafraid of failure, who do the best. If you can get yourself to relax and tell yourself you're doing fine, you'll improve your . . . success ten thousand percent. . . . People who can keep from panicking do a lot better than people who become nervous wrecks."

Believe in yourself. Even if you don't believe in yourself, if ☞ you make the interviewer think that you do, you'll be on the right track.

Irving Thalberg was the head of production at MGM during the ascendancy of Hollywood when he was a youthful twenty-five. He exhibited "a glacial calm" when confronted with the decisions involving millions of dollars he had to make day after day. His pictures were enormously successful and profitable. It was said that "Thalberg is always right." Did Irving Thalberg have confidence in himself? Did he ever doubt his judgment? This is what he confided to F. Scott Fitzgerald when he was at the height of his power:

Supposing there's got to be a road through the mountain and . . . there seems to be a half-dozen possible roads . . . each one of which, so far as you can determine, is as good as the other. Now suppose you happen to be the top man, there's a point where you don't exercise the faculty of judgment in the ordinary way, but simply the faculty of arbitrary decision. You say, "Well, I think we will put the road there," and you trace it with your finger and you know in your secret heart, and no one else knows, that you have no reason for putting the road there rather than in several other different courses, but you're the only person who knows that you don't know why you're doing it and you've got to stick to that and you've got to pretend that you know that you did it for specific reasons, even though you're utterly assailed by doubts at times as to the wisdom of your decision, because all these other possible decisions keep echoing in your ear. But when you're planning a new enterprise on a grand scale, the people under you mustn't ever know or guess that you're in doubt, because they've all got to have something to look up to and they mustn't ever dream that you're in doubt about any decision.

Everyone has doubts. Irving Thalberg had them. Julius Caesar had them. We all have them. But keep them hidden. You must exude confidence in who you are and what you say.

There are many ways to develop the appearance of confidence. Success breeds it. If you are offered some jobs, you'll begin to think that you're a pretty hot item, and you will enter interviews exuding it. But if you aren't made a lot of offers, **you can't let rejection erode your confidence in yourself.**

▶ The subject of the interview is you

☞ In developing confidence, you must recognize the things that tend to make you lack it. It is fear of the unknown that attacks and weakens your resolve. But there should be no such fear in being interviewed. **An interview is centered on the subject you know best: yourself.** The interview is much more of an unknown for the interviewer, and let's assume she's a woman. All she knows about you is what she has read on your résumé, which is generally all the preparation an interviewer will do.

If you have done your preparation, you know much more than the interviewer does. You know about her company. You might know something about her if you've been diligent enough to do some detective work. You also know that she is probably tired and perhaps bored. She's interviewed many people and gone through this routine time and again, asking the same questions and getting the same responses. She doesn't know what you're going to say, but you know what you want to say. So there is no reason for you not to feel confident. You're better prepared than the interviewer is. You know far more about the subject under discussion than she. The interview is yours.

▶ Advice of others can hurt your confidence

Confidence is often shaken by the advice of others. They'll tell you that you can't do this and that you shouldn't do that. They'll beat you down and get you to thinking negatively.

On December 12, 1900, a dinner party was given in New York City for the purpose of introducing Charles Schwab, a thirty-eight-year-old Pittsburgh steelman to the eastern banking establishment. Present were the kings of the financial world, including J. Pierpont Morgan.

The hosts of the dinner, J. Edward Simmons and Charles Steward Smith, advised Schwab that the other guests would not be receptive to a long speech and told him to keep any remarks he might wish to make to fifteen or twenty minutes.

Schwab knew what he wanted to say and he said it—for an hour and a half. And he kept his audience spellbound. After it was over, Morgan took him aside, and they conferred for another hour. The result was the formation of a steel trust that is known today as the U.S. Steel Company.

Had Schwab changed his mind in accordance with the advice given him by his hosts, he would not have achieved the enormous success that was his. He had the strength of character and confidence in himself to do what he had planned in spite of the warnings of his generous hosts.

▶ Effects of nervousness

Most interviewers expect a certain amount of nervousness on ☜ *the part of those interviewing for lower-level positions.*

Certainly a campus interviewer who is talking to students would think it normal that a student who has been through very few interviews in his life and has never held a full-time job would be nervous. Sweaty palms and nervous speech would be understood.

But if a person is being interviewed by the executive committee of a large corporation for the position as president of the corporation, nervousness would undoubtedly be a big mark against him. Someone interviewing for a position on a high level is expected to be confident. The exhibition of nervousness through a sweaty palm or forehead or a nervous tic would be an indication of a lack of confidence and would be noted. An interviewer may not consciously exclude the candidate for exhibiting such a human attitude, but the impression would almost certainly be such that the judgment the interviewer would make would be negative.

▶ How others handle nervousness

If you analyze nervousness, its causes and effects, you will recognize that it is a symptom of something else. In talking with successful people, two men with similar jobs told how they handle nervous feelings.

Joseph F. Alibrandi is the president of Whittaker Corporation. He has a grueling work schedule and a large load of responsibilities. He disdains nervousness and ways to combat it. "I don't look at the world that way," he says. "Sure, I get nervous, but that's part of doing it. See, the getting nervous is a symptom of the challenge of the problem. For me to sit back and work on curing the symptom just doesn't accomplish anything. What I've got to do is, there's something to be done and I've got to focus on getting that thing done. If there's nervousness as a symptom and perspiration and wet palms or whatever it is, that's fine, I'm not going to deal with those. They're just symptoms. I don't think there's a guy in the world who's not scared or what have you. I don't believe in Valium and all the other baloney. The problem is the problem and it's not going to change. If you've decided you've done everything you can do to optimize your probability to succeed, then you just jump in and do it."

Dr. Robert Langford, president of Bertea Corporation, looks at it this way. "My experience is that if you prepare yourself properly, you really don't have the time or inclination for the fright symptoms to appear.

"Since we're still dealing with human beings and there will be considerable gaps in their preparation, those things do occur. Among the things that I have found of some use is just before you come into the interview, give yourself some physical stress, even it it's only to the point of trying to run in place, or if you don't want to appear to be out of breath, do some isometrics of one sort or another. But do concentrate on the physical aspects, rather than the mental aspects just before an interview. Just point out to yourself that any time you spend any of your own personal energy on the symptoms, you're just wasting preparation that you should have.

"It's rather like trying to prepare for a classroom performance. There are all sorts of ways in which you can blow it. You can forget a half-hour of material that you have stored up in your head, which can certainly be done that night. You're much better off to say, 'Well, that's one circumstance about which there's very little control. My job here is to perform in as forceful a fashion to be of service to other people as possible.' You don't make yourself of service to somebody else if you're not relaxed, if you're not sensitive to other people's needs."

▶ Sweaty palms

Almost without exception, interviewers state that a sweaty palm is something that they overlook because they expect a certain amount of nervousness. The only exception to this rule is the situation where they are interviewing for a position that requires a great deal of self-confidence, such as president of a corporation or salesman.

However, despite the disclaimers, a sweaty palm is a very bad indication. It is distasteful to shake a hand that is wet. Even though the interviewer may be inclined to overlook the clamminess of your hand because he recognizes that it is merely a symptom of nervousness, the impression left is negative. The natural reaction to shaking a sweaty palm is to cringe. It causes you to start out the interview with a negative before you have uttered a word.

Some interviewers are honest enough to admit that sweaty palms can be a powerful factor in rejection. Leonard Zunin, in *Contact: The First Four Minutes,* states that one personnel director told him "that regardless of the qualifications of a man he interviews, 'If his handshake is weak and clammy, he's out.'" Zunin goes on to comment: "Such reaction to body language is probably far more prevalent than we realize, as others assume many things about our glance, stance, or advance."

An honest interviewer will candidly admit that a sweaty palm makes their skin crawly. Even though they may recognize it as a normal sign of nervousness, it creates a less than favorable initial impression. Dr. Carlotta Mellon, who was Appointments Assistant to former California Governor Edmund G. Brown, Jr., admits, "I react negatively to sweaty palms. People should try not to be so nervous. . . . They should probably have a handkerchief in hand to wipe their hands. . . . I think that sweaty palms convey a lack of confidence."

The general counsel of a major New York Stock Exchange corporation once told me of an interviewee who was so concerned by his sweaty palms that just before entering the interview, he went to wash his hands. Unfortunately he didn't dry them sufficiently, and when they shook hands, the general counsel felt cold moisture that he said "made me cringe."

No one would refuse to make an offer to a superstar because of sweaty palms, but why start out an interview with someone doing something that makes them cringe? It doesn't matter whether the moisture comes from nervous perspiration or insufficiently dried clean hands. Your first contact should be a positive one, and you should ensure that your hands are dry.

If you're nervous, no matter how many times you wash your hands or dry them off with a handkerchief, they'll still sweat. One method to reduce the moisture if you discover this problem is to sit with your palms exposed while you wait to be called into the interview. If you have your palms covered, whether they are in your lap or in your pockets, the heat will increase the sweating. If you allow the air to get at them, the moisture will be kept at a minimum. I have found that if I sit with my hands dangling down at my sides or sit with my palms in my lap but facing upward, sweaty palms cease to be a problem. These positions may feel awkward, but your interviewer isn't going to see you waiting, and what's important is that you not give him a wet hand when he offers his to you.

▶ How to combat nervousness

Nervousness attacks at different times, not just immediately prior to entering the interview room. Many people are so tense about an upcoming interview that they are unable to sleep the night before, tossing and turning and looking at the clock every ten or fifteen minutes.

Here are some suggestions for alleviating sleeplessness when the insomnia is caused by worry or tension.

1. Muscular relaxation. When you are worried about something, your mind continues to function and tenses the muscles. But you will not be able to sleep until you can relax your muscles. Dr. Walter Alvarez, the noted medical writer, suggests taking a warm bath if you feel that your body is tense. The heat tends to relax your muscles and make you drowsy.

2. Food or drink. Often people get sleepy after they eat. The physiological explanation may be that the blood rushes to your stomach to aid in the digestive process. Whatever the reason, sometimes a hot meal—or even a warm glass of milk—can cause drowsiness.

3. Alcohol. Although this is reputed to be the first step on the road to alcoholism, many people find that a glass of wine or beer before retiring allows them to relax and get to sleep quickly.

4. Drugs. Tranquilizers such as Valium and Librium are much in vogue as sleeping pills. Any drug such as this should not be taken unless a doctor has prescribed it. Even then, sometimes the side effects are worse than the cure. **It is not at all unusual for a tranquilizer to cause drowsiness the next morning and a lethargy that is difficult to shake quickly.** Unless you are experienced in taking such drugs, the night before a big interview is not the time to experiment just for the sake of getting to sleep. If you do ask your doctor for such a drug and plan on using it to ensure a good night's sleep before an interview, try it out a few nights before your interview so you know how it will affect you the next morning.

Milton in *Paradise Lost*, said, "The mind in its own place, and in itself, can make a Heaven of hell, and a Hell of Heaven." Shakespeare's Caesar said, "Cowards die many times before their deaths; the valiant never taste ,of death but once."

Both were making the same point. Worry avails you nothing. Preparation is the key to combatting nervousness. If you've prepared well, you should not have to worry. An interviewer is only asking you about yourself and no one on this earth knows that subject better than you. The best way to get to sleep is to forget the interview. By the night before the interview, you have done all that it is possible for you to do. If you haven't done all that you can, you may be justified in feeling guilty, but worry isn't going to allow you to do the preparation you feel you should have done. Just forget it and let it happen.

▶ You've got nothing to lose

Nervousness and lack of confidence are often caused by fear of losing. But what have you got to lose? People are nervous going into a job interview because they fear that they will not get an offer or be invited to return. **But before the interview they don't have an offer. If, after the interview they still don't have an offer, they are no worse off. So why worry?**

Throw caution to the wind. Look at the down side. What is the absolute worst that can happen to you? You won't get an offer. Well, right now you don't have an offer, so the down side is simply a maintenance of the status quo. That's nothing to worry about. Go into the interview forgetting about yourself. For fifteen minutes exude self-confidence. Take a chance. If you recognize that not getting that for which you hope is no disaster, you will be much looser and will try things that may work. If they don't you're no worse off.

When I was a young lawyer I had left a job with a law firm because I was intensely bored. After a summer of contemplation in Manhattan Beach, I decided that I wanted to work in a corporate law department. I made calls and wrote letters and finally got an interview with a vice-president and general counsel of a major airline company.

He was courteous, but at the end of the interview he said that he just didn't have enough work to justify another attorney. I returned home and wrote him a long letter volunteering to work for nothing. I told him that at that stage of my career the experience was worth more than the money. It was, truly, an outstanding letter, and I waited confidently for his reply. How could he possibly turn down such a magnanimous offer?

Well, I found out it was pretty easy for him to turn it down. He replied that he just didn't feel like he wanted to accept that responsibility. It can be crushing when someone tells you he doesn't want you to work for him for free! But I didn't let it dissuade me. I kept plugging and finally got a much better job. The point is that you've got to try. **If you see something you want, go after it in any way you can. You can't worry about rejection, and you can't let rejection get you down on yourself.**

I didn't hang my head and hide because of his refusal to hire me. I knew that I had done all that I could to get a job I wanted. I hadn't lost anything. Before I wrote the letter I didn't have the job. Afterward I still didn't have the job but I was no worse off. I had been honest and aggressive. If you do your best, if you take your best shot and still miss, you have nothing to feel badly about. I felt exhilarated. I knew I had fought the battle.

Don't look back

Eddie Rickenbacker was exposed to this attitude after he got the job with Frayer. He progressed to mechanic and, after building a racing car, it was entered in the Vanderbilt Cup, an elimination race among twelve American cars to determine the five American entrants. As mechanic, Rickenbacker rode in the car with Frayer, who was the driver.

Shortly after the elimination race began, the car developed engine trouble and had to drop out of the race. Frayer sat in the car for a "long moment" and then said simply, "We're through."

Rickenbacker was deeply impressed. He knew that an entire year of hard work had gone into preparation for entering the car in the Vanderbilt Cup and the car hadn't even survived the elimination race. Rickenbacker said, "I never forgot it. Gradually, over the years, the significance of that remark sank in, and I drew inspiration from it. To spell it out: TRY LIKE HELL TO WIN, BUT DON'T CRY IF YOU LOSE."

▶ Rejection may lead to a job

Rickenbacker's inspiration should be the motto for every interview. Interviewing is a terrible shock to the ego because it results in so many rejections. Even outstanding candidates will be rejected by the vast majority of interviewers. Even so, they eventually wind up with several offers. The odds in interviewing are long. If you receive favorable attention in one interview out of ten, you are doing well. That means that you must come to grips with rejection nine times out of ten attempts. You've got to keep your head high and find ways to compensate for the beating your ego must take.

But you never know where a rejection will lead. When I was in law school, many of my classmates and I wanted to work in Europe, but nobody did anything about it but dream. One day I wrote letters to thirty law firms throughout Europe asking for a summer job.

A month later some replies started dribbling in, mostly one-line letters of rejection. One man, Peter Crane, a London solicitor, was different. He wrote me a three-page letter telling me what it was like practicing law in London. He closed with a rejection, saying that they didn't hire summer clerks from America.

I wrote him back a thank-you letter. I felt that even though I had been unanimously rejected, I had learned something. But it didn't end there. Two years later I received another letter from Peter Crane saying that they had an opening for an American attorney and asking if I would be interested! From there I took a job that was the dream of probably every law student in America—working in a London solicitor's office!

Whenever you get down on yourself while going through the interviewing process, consider what Teddy Roosevelt had to say about trying and failing and trying again:

It is not the critic who counts, not the man who points out how the strong man stumbled and fell, or where the doer of deeds could have done them better. The credit belongs to the man who is actually in the arena: whose face is marred by dust, sweat and blood; who strives valiantly; who errs and comes short again and again . . . who knows the great enthusiasms, the great devotions and spends himself in a worthy cause; and at the best knows in the end the triumph of high achievement; and who, at the worst, if he fails, at least fails while daring greatly, so that his place shall never be with those cold and timid souls who know neither victory nor defeat.

 Relaxation

Relaxation is as important as any of the other techniques suggested in this book. But it almost needs to be treated with an admonition because the more one tries to achieve it, the further he tends to move in the opposite direction.

This virtue is important not only in interviewing but in virtually every endeavor you undertake. Above all, relax! That's easy to say. Here you're reading this book which emphasizes how important the selection interview is, and now you're told to relax. How in God's name can you relax when so much is riding on your interview?

The answer isn't easy, but it's one that each person must determine for himself. No matter what you try, you do it better if you're relaxed. Tennis players do much better when they're playing someone they know than when they're taking on the club champion. Suddenly their forehands are sailing into the fence, their backhands dribble off the frame, and they end up with the ball in their teeth while attempting to volley. Why? Because against their friend they are loose and aren't concerned with making mistakes. Against the club champion, mistakes are all they are thinking about. As a result, that's what they do: make mistakes.

Timothy Gallwey in his best-selling book *The Inner Game of Tennis*, advises his readers that the way to stop thinking mistakes on the tennis court is to concentrate on minutiae, such as focusing on the seams of the ball or saying "bounce" each time the ball hits the ground and "hit" each time the ball hits the racket.

▶ Judgments cause tension

Gallwey probes the reason why we become tense and make mistakes. **He says that it is the judgments that we make on ourselves that keep us from relaxing.**

What I mean by judgment is the act of assigning a negative or positive value to an event. . . . What is important to see here is that neither the "goodness" nor "badness" ascribed to the event . . . is an attribute of the [event] itself. Rather, they are evaluations *added* to the event in the minds of the players according to their individual reactions.

If you apply this to your everyday life you will discover its truth. If you simply observe something, you attach no value to it and you're totally relaxed.

But why do we make judgments? It's because when we do something, we expect certain results. If we don't achieve the desired result, then we make the judgment that it was bad. If we achieve the result we wanted, then we make the judgment that it was good.

In an interview, how can we keep ourselves from making judgments and then tying ourselves up in knots when we do not achieve our artificially imposed result?

View each interview as pragmatically as possible. Sure, you have a goal. But most people mistake their goal. Most of us going into an interview are completely inwardly directed. We say, "I'm going to an interview. I hope I get an offer." Already we've imposed a result upon the event that is not only not probable; it is not justified.

▶ You are interviewing them

☞ Remember what was said earlier: an interview is a two-way street. Certainly they are interviewing you to see if they want to offer you a job. But you are also interviewing them to see if you want to work for them. You are going to make some decisions on them, just as they will make some decisions on you. You must approach each interview with this frame of mind. If you do, you will eliminate the prime cause for tension: your artificially imposed objective of getting an offer. You don't know if you want an offer! **Go into the interview with the objective of finding out something about them.** Tell yourself, "I want to find out what it would be like to work for this outfit. Then I'll make a decision after I've gotten the data I need and thought about it for awhile."

If you take this approach to an interview, you'll find your frame of mind before an interview changes dramatically. No longer will you be worrying about your sweaty palms or what you say when you meet the interviewer. You won't be worrying about yourself. You'll be concerned about finding out about your interviewer and his company. You'll be outwardly oriented. You won't be setting objectives for your performance and the interviewer's evaluation. You won't be making **judgments** on your performance, so you'll be relaxed.

☞ When you are tense and you strain, your mind blocks and you don't respond in a normal manner. Don't worry about what you're going to say and how you're going to say it. If you have a general idea of what you want to cover, let it go at that and just be ready.

Years ago, Maxwell Maltz dealt with the mysterious effects of relaxation in his book *Psycho-Cybernetics:*

You must learn to trust your creative mechanism to do its work and not "jam it" by becoming too concerned or too anxious as to whether it will work or not, or by attempting to force it by too much conscious effort. You must **let it** work, rather than **make it** work. This trust is necessary because your creative mechanism operates below the level beneath the surface. Moreover, its nature is to operate **spontaneously** according to present need. Therefore, you have no guarantees in advance. It comes into operation as you act and as you place a demand upon it by your actions. You must not wait to act until you have proof—you must act as if it is there, and it will come through. "Do the thing and you will have the power," said Emerson.

Gallwey talks about this on the tennis court. He says that you must trust your inner self and "let it happen." If you're trying to be funny, you're not. If you're trying to be profound, you sound silly. Just relax and trust your normal reactions. An interview is, at its essence, the interrelationship between two people. One must react to the other.

Mean Joe Greene played defensive tackle for the Super Bowl champion Pittsburgh Steelers. The first half of the 1976 football season was a bad one for him. He played subpar football and the Steelers suffered, losing several games in a row.

Suddenly things turned around. Greene became the player he had been, and the Steelers, who had lost four of their first five games, won eleven in a row, allowing only twenty-eight points in their next nine games. What had caused the turnaround? "I was trying too hard not to make mistakes," Greene said. "In the past, I never gave a damn about mistakes. I used to play about 70 percent by design and 30 percent freelance. I'd take a chance now and then."

Once Greene forgot about himself and how he was performing, he resumed playing at the caliber he had achieved in the past. It was the thinking about what he wanted to do and worrying about mistakes that caused him to make the mistakes he was worrying about.

If you've done your homework and are prepared for the interview, you have nothing to fear. Basically the interviewer is going to ask you questions about yourself. What in the world could you know better than yourself? He can't ask a question that will stump you because he will limit himself to questions about your background and your ideas.

The Appendix in this book contains a list of questions that might be thrown at you in an interview. It's unlikely that an interviewer will come up with a question that is not at least touched upon in the list. So go into the interview confident that he's not going to throw something at you from left field.

Each person must find his own method of relaxing in potentially stressful situations. Even though the interview is important, it is not Armaggedon. Look upon it as an experience. Afterward, analyze how you reacted to his questions and try to determine how he reacted to you. If you can adopt a clinical approach to what's going to happen, if you can view it as a test from which you are going to improve yourself with new knowledge and awareness, you may tend to relax.

▶ How to relax

The process of being interviewed inevitably involves a period of waiting. This is the time when the most intense nervousness attacks. Your mind is racing a mile a minute trying to remember all the things you want to say and do. You're trying to keep your hands from sweating. You want to make sure your hair is not mussed, that your clothes are neat. Your heart is beating at a faster pace than normal. Your blood pressure is probably elevated. Above all, your mind is working overtime, telling you to check all the things you've previously thought of in preparing for the interview—and adding a few more.

Since it's too late to do any more preparation, you must relax your mind. This first step is to relax physically. Close your eyes and concentrate on relaxing each muscle in your body, beginning with your toes. Once your toes are relaxed, think about your ankles, then your calves, then your knees, then your thigh muscles, then your hips. Progress to your stomach muscles, your chest. Take some deep breaths. Then relax your neck. Lay your head back.

When your body is finally in a state of relaxation, cleanse your mind. Try to think of something calming and pleasant like a waterfall or the waves at the beach or a snowcapped peak with the deep blue sky beyond.

If you concentrate on relaxing your muscles and ridding your mind of all but pleasant thoughts, you should be able to feel the tension drain from your body. Your heartbeat will slow, the sweating will diminish, your mind will cease its race.

◗ Know when to stop preparing

In order to relax, you must cease your preparation before you go to the interview. As a student I recognized this when studying for exams in law school. I would completely drop out of everything three weeks preceding exams. I stayed in my room and spent the entire time memorizing my class notes, comprising hundreds of pages. I had a strict schedule that I followed religiously.

But one day before the date of my first exam, I put away all my notes. That day I played basketball or tennis. That night I went to a movie. Between exams I played basketball and went to movies. I did not return to my notes. I knew that I had studied enough either to know it or not. If I did not know it by then, it was too late to learn it. If I did know it, I couldn't know it any better. The most important thing for me at that time was to relax. I knew that my mind was trying to get me to check out this point or that point or to clarify something. The only way I could conquer this battle with myself was to throw myself into an activity totally unrelated to my courses. I worked on my jumpshot or forehand instead of the law. At night I further relaxed with James Bond or Audrey Hepburn. As a result, when I went into my exams, my mind was completely relaxed and the secret mechanism worked perfectly. I was confident that when I read the exam, my mind would perform and I let it.

It's the same with an interview. If you have done adequate preparation and you are relaxed, just let it work. You will react in accordance with your ability and preparation. As a result you will be yourself rather than something your mind is telling you you should be.

Maxwell Maltz has some things to say about relaxation that are to the point:

Conscious effort inhibits and "jams" the automatic creative mechanism. The reason some people are self-conscious and awkward in social situations is simply that they are too consciously concerned, too anxious, to do the right thing. They are painfully conscious of every move they make. Every action is "thought-out." Every word spoken is calculated for its effect. We speak of such persons as "inhibited," and rightly so. But it would be more true were we to say that the "person" is not inhibited; but that the person has "inhibited" his own creative mechanism. If these people could "let go," stop trying, not care, and give no thought to the matter of their behavior, they could act creatively, spontaneously, and "be themselves."

CHECKLIST

★ Continue to tell yourself that you are doing well.

★ Even if you don't believe in yourself, try to make the interviewer think that you do.

★ Keep your doubts to yourself.

★ An interview is centered on the subject you know best—yourself.

★ Don't let rejection erode your confidence.

★ The interviewer knows less about you than you do.

★ If you've done your preparation, you know more about him and his company than he knows about you.

★ Don't let the advice of others shake your confidence in yourself.

★ Interviewers expect a certain amount of nervousness.

★ Try to avoid sweaty palms by sitting with your palms exposed to air.

★ Combat nervousness by relaxing your muscles and getting enough sleep.

★ Look at the down side—before the interview you don't have an offer. The worst that can happen is that after the interview you still won't have an offer.

★ If you see something you want, go after it.

★ Don't worry about failure.

★ Don't look back.

★ Don't make tension-causing judgments.

★ Go into the interview with one of your objectives being that you are also interviewing the company to find out about it.

★ Trust yourself to react properly.

★ In order to relax mentally, you must first relax your body.

★ Stop preparing the night before the interview at the latest.

10

DRESS

The initial impression you make on the interviewer, and let's assume she's a woman, creates a presumption in her mind that has a strong effect on the rest of the interview. She looks at you and will react with an opinion derived from your appearance. How you are dressed will make up 80 percent of this opinion because it will be formed before you open your mouth.

We've all heard that the "clothes make the man." While this might not be true in an interview, the way in which you dress will certainly have an effect on the interviewer's initial impression of you. If there is something bizarre or slovenly about your dress, it may be a deciding factor in the result of the interview.

 You should dress in accordance with consideration for three factors: (1) dress to your advantage; (2) dress to suit your interviewer; (3) dress appropriately for the position for which you are interviewing.

Dress to your advantage

Dressing to your advantage means that you should not dress in a manner that will offend. Your choice of colors should blend well. If they do not, this will be a point that could stand out in your interviewer's mind to your detriment. Do you want to be remembered as "that person, wearing purple and pink"? A garish combination of colors will probably make more of an impression than any profound argument you make. How would you react if you were an interviewer and someone walked in wearing a red checked sports jacket, a purple striped shirt, and a pink polka-dot tie? Your lasting impression would probably be of the horrendous outfit he chose to wear and your confidence in his judgment would be permanently impaired.

Dress conservatively

For most positions, the safest bet is to dress conservatively. It is risky to wear new styles. Although even corporation presidents now sport long sideburns and hair over their ears, when the Beatles first wore their hair long, those who copied them were viewed as freaks. **It takes a long period of time for a fad to become a style. Wait until it's accepted before you adopt it for an interview.**

Dress for the interviewer

It is said that women dress for men. So, too, an interviewee should dress for the interviewer. If the interviewer is going to reach a conclusion on you, what you wear will be part of the facts she considers in reaching her conclusion. Don't dress to make some point about which the interviewer has no interest other than making a judgment on you because of the point you are choosing to make. Remember the story I referred to earlier of the law school student who came to an interview with me dressed in an old sweatshirt with holes in it, dirty blue jeans, and scuffed sneakers. **Don't try to make some childish point of being antiestablishment or independent by dressing in a manner that will offend your interviewer.** If you care enough to go to the interview, why blow it by dressing in a manner that tells the interviewer, "I don't give a damn about you"?

▶ Color

There is a great deal of disagreement as to whether color has any effect upon a person with whom you come into contact. If you dress for an interview as if you are going to a funeral, you'll be at a disadvantage with one who dresses like springtime unless your interviewer happens to be Dracula.

For what it's worth, the book *Color in Your World* treats the effect of colors upon the human psyche:

- If you like red, you are optimistic, restless, and passionate.

- If you like pink (and admit it), you are probably a woman. Among women, pink relates to "wealth, social advantage and to a sheltered, indulgent existence."

- If you like orange, you are good-natured but fickle, unsteady, and vacillating.

- If you like yellow, you are high-minded, introspective and contemplative, aloof, and given more to theory than action.

- If you like green you are affectionate, loyal, frank, and civic minded.

- If you like blue, you are deliberate and introspective, sensitive, and conservative.

- If you like brown, you are conscientious, shrewd, and obstinate.

- If you like grey, you are cautious and a compromiser.

- If you like black, you are sophisticated and dignified.

Obviously you are not going to be judged by an interviewer on as strict a scale as this. But these can be subconscious reactions to the colors you use in your dress.

Don't use this chart as a basis for dressing for interviews, but consider that some people do make judgments based upon appearance. Movies have educated us to expect certain professions when we see specific types of dress. A trench coat means a private detective. White tie on dark shirt means a gambler. Black leather jacket over a white tee shirt means a motorcycle tough.

I remember attending a meeting with a client who was looking for millions of dollars in financing. He had been told that the person with whom we were meeting had access to Arab money, so we set up a meeting with him at a restaurant in Los Angeles. When he showed up, I immediately sensed that we were wasting our time. He was dressed in a loud sports coat and a cravat. He hadn't uttered a word, but my reaction to him was that he was a flaky promoter.

Unfortunately, my initial impression proved to be accurate. We were forced to sit and listen to his pitch for over two hours, two hours of name dropping and grandiose schemes to finance my client's enterprise. I didn't say anything after he departed but asked my client what he thought. His reaction was instantaneous: "Two hours of nothing," he said.

☞ *Don't dress in a manner that will cause your interviewer to draw an unfavorable impression from your dress prior to starting the interview. If you stick to conservative dress, you're going to be safe.*

Because each interviewer is different, it's impossible to set down hard and fast rules about what to wear in an interview. Dr. Mellon, in reflecting the attitude of former California Governor Brown, says, "In our administration jeans are probably OK." But that would be taking a risk. You will always be safe if you dress conservatively and well.

▶ Scents

Other questions arise regarding grooming. If you're a woman, how much perfume, if any, should you wear? If you're a man, should you wear an aftershave? Scents are important. Remember that the interviewer is going through many interviews, and she may work in the room in which she interviews you. So you want to be sure that your scent doesn't linger after you.

If you wear perfume or aftershave or some other kind of lotion that emits an odor, there are two cardinal rules. First, make sure that none of it is on your hands so that it is not transferred to the interviewer when you shake hands. Second, be sure that it is not so strong that it will waft through her room the rest of the day. You don't want her to remember you because of a lingering smell, no matter how expensive the aroma.

▶ Dress for the job

There is another thing to be considered when it comes to your mode of dress. What kind of job are you interviewing for?

Although generally an interviewee should dress conservatively and should avoid extremes (such as micro-miniskirts and plunging necklines), this is not always true. For example, if a woman is interviewing for a position as a cocktail waitress, part of the qualification for the position may be sex appeal. Sharyn Cole says that she has interviewed women for positions as cocktail waitresses with their blouses unbottoned to their waist or with see-through blouses and no bra. She says that this dress doesn't result in a negative impression with her because she realizes that part of the job is sex appeal and that's one of the purposes of the interview: to display whether you've got it.

But no matter what kind of job you're interviewing for, you *should dress neatly. Even if you're interviewing to be a laborer or ditch digger, the person who dresses in a clean and neat manner will indicate by his dress that he at least had the interest in the job to take the time to dress well. It's never a plus to show up in dirty, unkempt clothes, no matter what the job.*

▶ Sexy dress

Depending upon what kind of job you're interviewing for and how you want the job to work out, your dress can vary, with one exception: sexy dress is frowned upon by most interviewers.

One attractive woman who worked her way up to executive secretary to the chief executive of a major corporation, always dressed conservatively. Although she did not downplay her physical attractiveness, she did not dress in a manner that would flaunt it. Her objective was to get a good position for which she felt her secretarial skills qualified her.

Not every woman who wants to be a secretary has the required skills of shorthand, typing, and office management. There are a lot of people looking for jobs for which they are unqualified. If you are honest enough with yourself to recognize your shortcomings, it may be to your advantage to dress to accentuate your sex appeal. Your interviewer, and in this case let's assume he's a man, may be more interested in sensuality than efficiency.

If he isn't, however, be prepared to be asked about the way you have chosen to dress for the interview. Invariably sophisticated interviewers with whom I have spoken say that if a woman comes in for an interview obviously dressed to accentuate her feminine allure, they ask her why she came dressed like that.

If she answers that she knows she's attractive and she felt that since she was interviewing with a man for a job it would give her an advantage, the response in the interviewer is generally negative. The one answer most interviewers agree would spark a positive response is, "This is the way I dress. This is me."

▶ Women in management

Attractive women who are interviewing for positions in management have different problems. One Los Angeles attorney who has worked for a major Wall Street law firm and a major NYSE corporation is a bright and attractive woman. She says: "I'm a fanatic on how women should dress for an interview. I never wear pants and I always wear very conservative dresses, on the long side, never anything short, never anything low cut, never anything too flamboyant. Most of my things are solid colors. I dress in pastels or navy and black and brown. It's hard to tell me from a secretary anyway. If I go in dressed too much like a secretary, I get taken for a secretary. It also makes me look more professional. I want to look good in what I buy. I certainly don't tie my hair back and wear horned-rim glasses and no makeup. But I think it looks more professional and businesslike and gains me better acceptance to dress conservatively."

She varies this theme, however, when interviewing with someone nearer her own age. "When I know I'm going to be interviewing a man who is close to my own age, I try to wear something softer, like a baby blue or a light green, maybe even a pink because it makes me seem less threatening to him. It looks more feminine. It looks softer. It looks less professional and therefore he feels less challenged by me."

She has had several interviewing experiences where the combination of her sex and aggressiveness cost her offers. One firm made her an offer and then withdrew it; the younger members in the firm argued that she threatened to wreck the close, noncompetitive atmosphere they had created in the firm. She combats this feeling by looking more feminine and therefore less aggressive when she interviews younger men.

She puts a large emphasis on colors. Her experience has proven to her that the way she dresses has a very important effect on the interview.

Cleanliness

There is one constant that applies to both men and woman. No matter what your sex and no matter what type of job you are interviewing for, be neat and clean.

Be sure that your fingernails are properly cut and clean. Dirty fingernails can result in a feeling of revulsion in an interviewer that can cause a negative feeling you will be unable to counter.

Ensure that your hair is neat. If you have to park outside the building where you are having your interview, the wind may mess up your hair. Try to visit a restroom and inspect your coiffure before going into your interview.

Your clothes should be neat and pressed, and your shoes should not be scuffed.

Women should be very careful about the amount of jewelry they wear. If you're interviewing for a secretarial position, an armful of bracelets and a handful of rings can leave a negative impression.

If you are bothered by bad breath, take a breath mint before entering the interview. If your interview is in the afternoon, don't have a cocktail at lunch. The smell of liquor on the breath will not be received favorably. Also be careful of what you eat before your interview. If you eat Italian food, for example, you may come across as one huge garlic clove to your interviewer.

Be sure you bathe before the interview. There is probably no bigger turnoff for an interviewer than to interview someone who has body odor. If you've got this problem more severely than others, try and bathe just before leaving for the interview and use a deodorant-antiperspirant.

Your clothes should be fresh. If you have a suit, shirt, or dress that you've worn once and feel that you can get another wearing out of it before sending it to the cleaners, get the additional wearing some other time. If you wear freshly cleaned and pressed clothes, you won't have to worry about your clothes being spotty, wrinkled, or smelly.

Robert H. Lentz, vice-president and chief counsel for Litton Industries, sums it up well: "Personal appearance and personal habits are very important. If they have bad breath or body odor I'd say that it implies a certain sloppiness that's personal. I think that there's an inference of some value that if a person is sloppy in appearance or has a greasy tie, for example, or a very cavalier outfit going out for a job interview, it implies that the person is possibly sloppy in many ways. I would consider that a very definite negative. I think that personal appearance is highly important. **Even though it's a first impression, people have to realize that when they're being interviewed they're trying to convey as much as possible to the interviewer in a very limited amount of time.** Proper dress and good personal appearance are both important."

CHECKLIST

★ Dress to your advantage.
★ Dress to suit your interviewer.

* Dress for the position for which you are interviewing.
* Your colors and patterns should coordinate.
* Dress conservatively.
* Consider the effect your choice of colors will have.
* Don't use too much perfume or aftershave.
* Women should not dress sensually unless sex appeal is part of the job.
* Your fingernails should be clean and properly cut.
* Your hair should be neat and combed.
* Check out your appearance in a mirror before entering the interview.
* Your clothes should be fresh, neat, and pressed.
* Your shoes should not be scuffed.
* Your jewelry should be sparse.
* If you have bad breath, take a breath mint.
* Don't drink liquor before an interview.
* Don't eat foods that will leave an odor on your breath before an interview.
* Bathe and use a deodorant-antiperspirant before the interview.

11

SILENCE AND POWER

In the late nineteenth century, Adrian (Cap) Anson was the premier baseball player in the National League. He batted over .400 and fielded flawlessly. But one thing bugged Anson, and in 1888 he did something about it.

Anson organized a group of fellow baseball players and demanded that blacks be prohibited from playing in the National League. Because of his prestige and the tenor of the times, an unwritten law was maintained, and thereafter not a black player's name graced the box scores of the major leagues, despite such standout players as Josh Gibson, Satchel Paige, and James (Cool Papa) Bell.

In 1945 a grizzled baseball executive had a plan. Branch Rickey was general manager of the Brooklyn Dodgers, and he told his scout, Clyde Sukeforth, to go to Chicago, check out a player's arm and, if satisfied that his arm was sound, bring him to Brooklyn for an interview.

Sukeforth returned a few days later, and he and Jackie Robinson entered Rickey's office. Sukeforth told Rickey that he hadn't seen Robinson's arm but had brought him in for Rickey to interview anyway.

After introductions, Rickey subjected Robinson to intense study. No one said a word as Rickey stared at Robinson for several minutes. Finally Rickey told Robinson that for years he had been looking for a great black baseball player, that he had a feeling that Robinson was his man. But he said that he needed someone who was more than a great athlete; he needed someone who could take insults and abuse and have the courage not to fight back. He described the terrible abuse that Robinson would have to take from everyone—fellow players, fans, sports writers, even his own teammates. But Rickey said if the first black man to play baseball in the National League in fifty years fought back, he'd set the cause back twenty years.

When Rickey was through, he waited for Robinson's response. But Robinson didn't say anything. For five minutes the room was enmeshed in silence as Robinson thought and Rickey waited. Sukeforth said that Rickey was immensely impressed that Robinson did not give a quick answer.

Finally Robinson told Rickey that he had no doubts about his ability to play baseball in the National League but that that judgment would be up to Rickey. He promised that if Rickey were willing to take the risk there would not be any incident. Thus ended a classic interview, one that changed not only the complexion of the sporting world but the opportunities of blacks in all professions.

Jackie Robinson was a man of power, as was Branch Rickey. Their initial meeting emphasizes the manifestation of power through silence. Note that each used silence; and note the other's response.

▶ Silence by the interviewer

When they first met, Rickey said nothing, staring at Robinson for several minutes. Rickey was applying stress before he uttered a word. Robinson responded by withstanding the scrutiny with silence and confidence. It was Rickey's move. Had Robinson fidgeted or shown discomfiture, probably Rickey's impression would have been less favorable. Rickey had been looking for forty years to break the color line. A few more years wouldn't matter. He had to have the man who could stand the tension under which he would be put. He had to have a man of power and restraint.

▶ The thinking silence

After Rickey had put the facts before Robinson, Robinson was silent. He had the confidence in himself to think the problem through, and he wasn't intimidated by the powerful man across the desk from him. The room was filled with silence for five minutes. Someone who is uncomfortable with himself, or is intimidated, or lacks confidence, will find five minutes of silence in the same room with a man of power and decision an eternity. But Robinson thought the problem through. He didn't rush out with a rapid acceptance, which could have been his undoing. **He thus showed Rickey that he had the confidence in himself to consider the proposition as something that could expose him to great risk and that he wasn't going to jump at an opportunity without considering the consequences.**

☞   Each of these men conveyed his power to the other through silence. Although Rickey used silence as a tool, Robinson was not trained in interviewing and was reacting from within. His silence was a genuine indication of the man inside.

Most people tend to think it is their obligation to fill gaps in conversation. They feel an urge to talk when there is silence. But sometimes silence on the part of an interviewer invites initiative by the interviewee. Other times it does not. It's important to recognize one from the other.

Silence you should not break

In the Robinson-Rickey interview, it was clear that Rickey's initial silence did not invite conversation from Robinson. It's very rare that in an employment interview a candidate will be met with such a stressful imposition of silence upon introduction.

If you are alert, you may be able to distinguish an invitation from an evaluation. In **Contact: The First Four Minutes,** authors Leonard and Natalie Zunin say, "Once people are talking, they look at their partners less often than when they listen. To look away while speaking is natural. . . . A pause while glancing away usually means an incomplete phrase, signaling, 'I have not yet said all I want to say; don't interrupt.'"

Silence you should break

Often silence does invite initiative. I remember an interview I had with a potential client. The president of the company was fairly shy. I accompanied the vice-president to the president's office and the interview consisted mostly of my talking with the vice-president while the president observed.

Nobody asked me questions. We were introduced, and the three of us just sat there looking at one another. It was clearly an invitation for me to take over the interview, so I started discussing a real estate project upon which I was working, which I had discussed previously with the vice-president. We chatted about this, and then I slowly introduced other areas in which I had worked that I felt were germane to the operations of the company.

The president hardly uttered a word. After I felt that I had established my credentials, I asked the president to tell me something about his company and its problems and why he felt that he needed a lawyer.

The dichotomy between the initial silence in this situation and the Robinson-Rickey silence was determined by the ambience of the confrontations. There was nothing friendly about the Rickey silence. It was plainly evaluative. On the *other hand, the silence that greeted me in the president's office was expectant. Had Robinson started to talk while Rickey was staring at him, or had I remained silent while the president waited, we each would have misjudged the situation and most probably blown the interview.*

The proper handling of silence is one of the best exhibitions of power and self-confidence you will ever find in an interview. If you get into a silence situation and use it properly, you can't help but win. Very few interviewees know how to react to silence, and if the interviewer knows what he's doing and you know what you're doing, your feeling of having handled the situation properly will be instantaneous.

▶ Don't retract

Silence as an interviewing technique is simple. Sometime around the middle of the interview, the interviewer will ask a question requiring a short answer. He gets the short answer. Then he doesn't respond. Nothing. He just sits there, looking at you but saying nothing.

What's he doing? You hastily review your answer and retract or qualify it. If you do that, you've made a mistake. DON'T RETRACT! Don't change what you've said for the reason that you think he might disagree with you.

A small digression here may emphasize this point. It is said that in the first year of law school, the professors try to scare you to death. Law school is generally taught by the Socratic, or question and answer, method where the professor quizzes a student about a case the class has read. The professor will get the student to take a stand and then caustically tear the position to shreds.

Contracts Professor Richard Speidel was feared at Virginia Law School for his brutality to the students' psyches. It was the rule rather than the exception that he would keep a student standing for the entire hour, grilling him on points of contract law. Sometimes he would start the next class with the person who had been destroyed the previous session, so you could never relax.

But there was a rule to Speidel's game, and it is a cardinal rule that is also applicable to interviewing: if you stuck to your guns and didn't change your position when he attacked you, he'd let you sit down after about fifteen minutes.

One day he called on me and had me brief a case about a crew of a merchant ship who agreed to ship out for a certain rate; when the ship hit the high seas, the crew struck for three times the rate previously agreed upon.

"Well, Mr. Medley," said Mr. Speidel, "what would you do if the ship's owner called you for advice?"

"I'd tell him to go ahead and agree to pay the rate and then renege when the cargo was unloaded at destination," I replied.

"What!" exploded Speidel. "You'd have the ship's owner make a commitment he never had any intention of honoring?"

"Well," I countered, "I'd say that he was acting under undue duress and that he wasn't bound because the crew's actions were in breach of contract."

"Do you mean, Mr. Medley, that he honor only the commitments he wants to honor, those that work to his advantage, and ignore those that work to his disadvantage? What is this, Mr. Medley," he attacked with devastating vitriol, "the two-edged sword of Damocles?"

He leaned against the blackboard and waited. Well, I thought, he's certainly got a good point. Maybe I should reconsider. Maybe he'll like me better if I agree with him and will treat me more easily. But then I remembered how he had changed and destroyed people before. If I change, he'll start arguing what I'm arguing now. If I backtrack, he'll keep switching and I'll never sit down. Taking a deep breath, I gambled on a little show of strength and confidence in my position. "Not for my client," I replied. "He would be sticking by the original agreement."

He glared for a minute and then, with a smirk, said, "You may sit down, Mr. Medley." My ordeal for the year was over; it had lasted less than ten minutes.

When silence is used as a method of challenging your belief in your statements, you can be devastated. If you are faced with this situation and if you've taken a position, don't backtrack. Just sit and wait. Generally in an interview it's not what you say when you voice your opinions; it's whether you have confidence in them.

▶ Don't mutter

A second mistake that is made in the face of silence is to start to mutter. You may have given an opinion and the interviewer just sits there looking at you. So you add something on to it. He still says nothing, so you add something else.

☞   If you've said what you have to say on a subject, stop. If he doesn't immediately pick up the conversation, you have no obligation to continue talking. If you've made an initial assessment that the interviewer knows what he's doing and that you aren't in the position of helping him out to keep the conversation flowing, then you should recognize his introduction of stress. Muttering and frivolous talking in the face of silence indicate a lack of confidence and the fact that the tension he has created is getting to you. So don't add taglines to your opinions. If you're through talking on a subject, let it be.

▶ Just wait calmly

☞ Silence is easy to handle if you recognize it quickly for what it is: a ploy. The interviewer is testing you. The best way to survive it is to sit calmly and wait for him to continue the interview. Don't fidget. Don't look down or around. Just sit and look at him expectantly. The silence cannot last long because the interview is for a short period of time, and there are many things he wants to cover. If you're not ready for the silence, it may seem to last an eternity. If you are prepared and recognize it, it will be over in a few seconds and you may have conveyed more than you could have with thousands of words.

A sophisticated interviewer will introduce stressful silence at a time when you least expect it. If you are prepared for it and handle it properly, you will get one of the warmest, positive feelings you'll ever receive out of an interview. If you remember what has been said here and if you're relaxed and confident, you should be able to handle stressful silence whenever it's introduced.

▶ Silence by the interviewee

The interviewee can use silence as a technique in answering. If you give a quick answer, for example, you may leave a bad impression. The way you answer a difficult question may convey more than the answer itself. An answer given too quickly, without sufficient thought, may lead the interviewer to think you are a person of little depth.

The Robinson-Rickey interview illustrates this point too. Perhaps the most important aspect of Rickey's evaluation was the fact that Robinson sat silent for five minutes before answering. Remember, Rickey had not offered him a job. He had merely said, "I have reason to believe that you're [my] man." Unquestionably the manner of Robinson's response was what decided the day. Had Robinson said without a pause that he wanted the job, Rickey undoubtedly would have concluded that Robinson either did not recognize the turmoil into which he would be entering or was insincere in his promise to avoid incidents.

But Robinson thought through what he had just heard. By his silence, he conveyed to Rickey the fact that he recognized the risks and the tremendous self-control that would be required of him.

Look at it from Rickey's viewpoint. Black ballplayers had been yearning for over fifty years to get into organized baseball. He was making an offer that thousands of black men had dreamed of for a half-century. Rickey knew that Robinson was no different from any other black ballplayer. He wanted to play in organized baseball, where the money and fame were. But Rickey had to be convinced that Robinson recognized the risks involved and what would be required of him.

The fact that Robinson did not jump for the plum but thought about it for a long period before replying convinced Rickey probably even before he heard the answer that Robinson was his man. It was the silence, not the words, that did it.

There are two ways for an interviewee to handle silence introduced into an interview as an imposition of stress. The first is to sit expectantly. The second involves a risk and must be handled adroitly. If you have finished your answer to one of the questions and the interviewer just sits and stares, you recognize that stress has been introduced. **Who should break the silence? If you break it, do so only by asking a question.**

As we have seen, changing your statement or backtracking or muttering can be interpreted as a lack of confidence in yourself and what you have said. If a few seconds pass and you know the interviewer is using silence as stress and not just thinking over your answer or preparing a new question, you may ask, "Do you mind if I ask you a few questions about your company [or the job or yourself]?" This breaks the silence in an acceptable manner without revealing any insecurity on your part or any inability to handle the silence. It also takes the silence away from him as a weapon.

By asking a question pertinent to the interview, you are telling the interviewer that you recognize that the interview is for a finite period of time and you want to cover as many areas as possible. There is quite a bit of information you wish to obtain from him, and this seems like a good spot in the interview to get it. You tacitly don't recognize his imposition of stress for what it is. Instead you are telling him, "Well, if you're through, there are some things I'd like to ask."

Just remember: if you break the silence, don't do it by volunteering more information, either on the subject just finished or on a different subject. If you do, you will indicate a lack of ability to deal with the silence, and this can be a big negative. If you have communicated by your method of speaking that you have finished talking on the subject under discussion (which is generally done by pausing and looking at the interviewer), you must keep it closed. By bringing the subject up again in response to the silence, you will probably have failed the silence test. Similarly, by bringing up an entirely new subject after you have signaled that you have finished speaking, you express your insecurity. After you have indicated that you've finished speaking, don't begin again unless it's to ask some questions.

▶ How to endure stressful silence calmly

Silence is a powerful phenomenon that can produce intriguing effects. When an interviewee unexpectedly encounters silence, the predictable result is that the silence will cause him to think about his frailties. The interviewee will begin to worry that he has said the wrong thing, perhaps that his nose is running, her blouse is becoming unbuttoned, or hair is out of place. So without thinking, the interviewee will rush to correct whatever it is that is worrying him. He may restate something he's said, wipe his nose, feel to see that her blouse is okay or brush the hair back. All of these actions are telltale signs of insecurity in the face of silence.

Since the cause of the insecurity is derived from an active mind, the cure is to keep your mind busy with other matters. You know that the best way to handle silence is simply to return the interviewer's stare with a calm, anticipatory look. If your mind is racing trying to determine which weakness he's focusing on, you're going to fidget by going directly to your supposed weakness. The solution is to keep your mind too busy to think about your weaknesses.

The best way I have discovered to do this is to become aware of the silence and see how long it lasts. The moment that you recognize that the interviewer is imposing silence, start counting to yourself to see how long it lasts. I'll guarantee that it won't be longer than fifteen seconds. Start counting to yourself "one thousand-one, one thousand-two" and so on until he breaks the silence. You'll be so busy ensuring that your one-thousands actually equal one second that your mind won't focus on your runny nose or open blouse. Your demeanor will reflect a calm anticipation, and suddenly your test will be over and the interviewer will continue the interview by breaking the silence with another question.

▶ Silence as a plea for help

Since interviewers are often more nervous than the interviewee, you must recognize when you are talking with a sophisticated interviewer or an inexperienced one so that you can distinguish a stressful silence from a plea for help.

In a lecture I gave at UCLA on being interviewed, one of the students asked what to do when the interviewer didn't say anything. He said he had been in several interviews where there were long silences, and he didn't know what was expected of him. If the interviewer is inexperienced, he may be thinking only of how to get through the interview without having long pauses. It is simple to determine whether a silence is an intentional imposition of stress or whether the interviewer can't think of anything to say.

One of the keys to look for in making this determination is whether the interviewer looks at you. If he does and says nothing, he is obviously introducing stress, and you should act accordingly. If, on the other hand, he looks away, fidgets, or exhibits other nervous mannerisms, he probably can't think of anything to say and is wondering how he's ever going to get through this interview.

Don't delude yourself by thinking that this situation never happens. Many selection interviewers **are** inexperienced, and more than you might imagine are terrified of interviews. They are on uncertain ground, and a lot of them are just as worried that they are going to make fools of themselves in front of you as you are that you're going to make a fool of yourself in front of them.

In such a situation, you should come to the interviewer's rescue by telling him you have some questions. He will undoubtedly ask to hear them, and you can then inquire about the job, the company or himself. He should feel relief and indebtedness to you for saving him from embarrassment and for not exposing his inexperience.

CHECKLIST

★ Silence by the interviewer is generally an imposition of stress.

★ Silence by the interviewee is a manifestation of confidence.

★ Don't break a stressful silence imposed by the interviewer except to ask a question.

★ The interviewer will cue you as to when he wants you to break the silence.

★ If the silence is not imposed as stress, it's your obligation to break it.

★ Don't retract in the face of silence.

★ Don't mutter in the face of silence.

★ Wait through a stressful silence by counting the seconds it lasts.

★ Don't fidget through a stressful silence.

★ If you recognize that the interviewer is inexperienced and his silence is a plea for help, break it by asking questions.

12

SEX

There are male bosses who are looking for sexy employees for their extracurricular benefits. If you're an attractive woman and you're interviewing for a job, you must analyze yourself very candidly to determine what you want and what you have to offer.

Most counselors will advise that sex in the office is a bad thing and that if you get a job because of it, everything will turn out poorly. Barbara Walters in her book, *How to Talk with Practically Anybody About Practically Anything,* says, "When to be sexy, and when not. When not is when applying for a job, or when trying to keep one. . . . The beddable look does not lead to the door marked **President,** but to the one marked **Exit.** Be sexy on your own time; working hours and job interviews require the crisp and cool version of you."

▶ Candidly assess what you have to offer

If you happen to be Barbara Walters—attractive, intelligent, confident, articulate, and ambitious—this is good advice. But if you're someone else and are only attractive and ambitious, you've got to examine how you're going to get a job. Maybe the only thing you have to offer is the fact that you are attractive. Maybe you can't fill many jobs because you don't have the skills required. If this is so, you should emphasize what you've got to offer: your attractiveness. The Walters theory is based on the hypothesis that all interviewers are professional and are looking only for someone who can do the job. This may be true in a great many cases, but there are many interviewers who have a more hedonistic outlook on life. A top corporate executive told me of one success story that defied the Walters theory in all respects:

"When I was a young manager," he said, "I had just joined a division and had to hire a secretary. I was sent one of the most beautiful, sensuous women I had ever seen. She was an absolute knockout. I interviewed her and while she played games with her eyes, I had enough self-control to determine that she couldn't type very well, wasn't very good at shorthand, didn't seem to be very well organized, and had very little experience in what I needed for a person to run my office. Reluctantly I told her that I didn't think she qualified for the job.

"She was a friend of the person in charge of secretarial employment so she got a job as a typist. Whenever an executive was looking for a secretary, she was the first one to be interviewed. Finally, after work one day, she met an executive who had one of the most efficient secretaries in the office. But this executive was the man for whom she was looking. He looked into her eyes and fired his secretary the next day.

"She worked for him for several months, he became very morose because his work fell off, she received an offer to become secretary to the president of another company and left. She found a home as a 'window dressing' secretary to a company president who had others to do the real work. The last I heard everyone was happy except the guy who originally hired her. He never could find someone who managed his office the way his first secretary did."

It's true that there is a much diminished chance that a job obtained on the basis of sexual attractiveness will last as long as one based upon ability. You should recognize the pitfalls if you are going to base your strategy on this.

Walters thinks that office affairs inevitably lead to problems: "Most bosses are married men and so, unless it turns out to be for keeps and he goes the whole route of divorcing his wife and marrying you, the only way to end the affair will be to fire you."

▶ Changing jobs

☞ *If you get your job because of sex, once the sexual attraction ceases, your performance will be subjected to the spotlight of attention. If you're not performing in your job and there is no more sexual attraction, you're probably going to be back in the job line pretty soon. If you enter on this path, you must change jobs pretty regularly.*

The woman referred to above was wise; she made her move to a better job while she still had good credentials. Also her boss was beginning to cool on her and, given his mental outlook, it was easier for him to give a good recommendation to get rid of her than to be truthful to the prospective employer and then fire her.

If all you have to offer is sex, and you decide that this is the route you're going to take, be sure you know the rules of the game, but be prepared to ride the roller-coaster.

▶ Women's reactions

Because of their sex, the question of sexual attractiveness and ulterior motives is a difficult one for many women who are interested in a career. Some women have a chip on their shoulder concerning their femininity. This is somewhat understandable; it is not unusual for an attractive woman to be offered opportunities in an interview that are not job related. To an intelligent, ambitious woman, this can be offensive. But women must develop the ability to distinguish between a proposition and a compliment.

I once interviewed a beautiful woman at a major law school who was a good student, articulate and sensuous. After the videotaping was completed, she lingered to ask some questions about job opportunities. I told her that since she was such an attractive woman, she would not want for job offers.

She reacted with intense hostility. "Well," she huffed, "I hope they're interested in me for other reasons!" and stormed out of the room. She had taken a sincere compliment so poorly that she made me feel terrible.

Walters quotes Dr. Benjamin Spock in a passage that every woman in the job market should remember. He says that people should have "sufficient sexual and romantic maturity to allow a person—man or woman—to show, whenever he is dealing with a member of the opposite sex, that he is pleasantly aware of [the other person's sexual attractiveness] and that he can be appropriately attentive and charming, without implying an intention of further seductiveness."

There is little that is more offensive to a man than to have a well-intended compliment to a woman flung in his face. If you want to blow an interview, act as did the young lady I complimented. She turned an asset into a liability. If you think about it, your looks are just as important an asset as your brains or your grades or your experience. If you are a sensuous person, why downplay it?

The job market is a difficult field at best. In days of rising unemployment and expanding availability of workers, any asset you have should be used. Sex must be used subtly, but it should not be ignored. If you've got it, don't flaunt it, but let it work.

▶ Evaluate the interviewer's objective

There is another possibility that should be covered here, and it calls for you to make a pragmatic evaluation of the interviewer.

If you are attractive, intelligent, articulate, and ambitious and are being interviewed by a person of the opposite sex, there may come a time when you feel you are being pursued for your sexual attractiveness rather than your capabilities. It may not be because of something overt; it will just be a feeling that you have. What should you do? Should you bring it out in the open? Should you react with indignation? Should you accept an offer?

Don't follow the first two alternatives. Your intuition may be wrong, and to bring the question of sex out in the open or react with indignation would result in an insult and almost certain withdrawal or lessening of interest.

In this situation, you must both analyze yourself and evaluate the interviewer. If you have conducted a good interview yourself, you should have gained some insight into the interviewer to make a judgment. Is he a professional, or does he have hedonistic leanings?

If you're not sure whether he's interested in you because you're capable or because you're sexy, but you conclude that even though he may have hedonistic leanings and ulterior motives, he's still a professional and will recognize and reward accomplishment, and if you're confident you can do the job, you should leave your doubts unspoken and pursue an offer.

If your intuitions prove correct and he did have ulterior motives, you can disabuse him in a tactful way after you have the job. In the meantime, if your performance has been good, you should have won a respected place in the organization. You may never be sure that the offer was not made because of sex, but what difference does it make? So long as you respect his professionalism and can handle the sexual advances when they come, you have achieved your objective—a job—and the fact that you may have gotten it because you're attractive is irrelevant. You should trade on what you have and use all your assets.

If, on the other hand, you do not gain a measure of respect and confidence in the interviewer's professionalism, you should trust your intuition and turn down the interest. A job that is taken on the basis of sex, when you want it on the basis of capability, can lead only to disaster if you don't want to participate in sexual games and he's not professional enough to recognize your talent in spite of your unwillingness to play with him. In this situation, trust your intuition and move on to more interviews with others.

▶ Requests for dates

Another problem for a woman is that the interviewer may become attracted to her and want to ask her out. One interviewee put it this way: "I'm here applying for a professional job. My feeling is that it shouldn't impinge on your personal relationship at all. That bothers me quite a lot, by injecting it into the situation. When it occurs, I say, 'Well, maybe we should talk about that later.' I'd try to focus on what we're there for, which is finding out about their company and my qualifications."

Another woman says, "If it's brought up in a subtle way, I try to ignore it and give them the opportunity to ignore it also. Generally they don't just come out and ask for a date. They do it more subtly. One interviewer said, 'Gee, you look kind of pale. Don't you like to get out in the sun?'

"I said, 'I like the sun.'

"He said, 'Don't you go swimming?'

"I said, 'Yeah.'

"He said, "Well, I have a swimming pool. You ought to come over and go swimming at my place.'

"That's when I'll just tend to ignore it by saying, 'Well, I don't like swimming much' or something like that.

"Most of the men I've dealt with are married, so they're not likely to come right out and ask, 'Will you go out with me?' They're usually more likely to test the water in a roundabout fashion, which gives them the opportunity to pretend there was nothing if you react negatively."

She continued, "That type of situation would make me hesitate quite a bit because I would assume that anybody who would bring that up in the interview situation would certainly bring it up in a working situation. It seems to me in an interview situation, you're portraying what you think is most important about yourself and what you want to be considered by the other person."

Another woman talked about whether to deal with the problem directly: "If I were inclined to be impressed by the company, I'd estimate what the chances were of my working with the interviewer. If they were slim, I probably wouldn't say anything. If, on the other hand, my inclination was negative anyway, I'd probably say that I didn't feel that that had any relevance to what we're dealing with. But that wouldn't be enough to make me pull out of a job I really wanted."

▶ Questions about a man's marital status

Occasionally a single man will be asked if he's going with someone or contemplating marriage. Whereas women are ready for questions about their child-bearing desires and their husbands, men are generally caught by surprise by this sort of question. If you are interviewing for a higher-level position, many companies feel that a wife can be a definite factor in a man's career. They therefore sometimes want to meet the wife or fiancé to assess her and how she will affect her husband's performance. Recognize that the question may be asked and the purpose behind it. Otherwise it can catch you unaware, and your reaction may be one of stupefaction or defensiveness, which can jeopardize the success of the interview.

▶ How a job acquired by sex appeal turned to disaster

One executive told me, "I learned my lesson about sex very early. The first secretary that I hired by myself was a gorgeous woman who didn't have much to offer other than sensuality.

"She had red hair and green eyes and a body that would stop traffic on Broadway. She showed up for her interview in a miniskirt and tight sweater. I was overwhelmed. I offered her the job and, although it was fun to dictate to her, her performance was something else.

"She started out playing it her way. She was married, and the thought of anything extracurricular was the farthest thing from my mind. But I took her out to lunch once and when I helped her out of the car, she gave my hand the tiniest little squeeze, letting me know she was available. Although I never did follow it up, I continued to enjoy her beauty and flirtatiousness.

"But my work wasn't getting out. I found out later that she would ask the other girls in the office to help her with her typing and that she was an irritant to everyone, which affected my ability to perform without my knowing it. People were beginning to resent me. But I was young and naive and didn't realize this, except for a vague uneasiness that all was not as it should be.

"Finally some friendly secretaries began to tell me what was going on and I had my first great trauma. I had to fire her. I moped about how to do it. I was not too friendly to her and didn't participate in her reparté and finally she was sitting in my office one day and I told her she'd have to get another job.

"'You can't fire me,' she said. 'I won't let you.'

"Getting rid of her was harder than killing a swarm of locusts.

"Finally, six weeks later she was gone, but not forgotten. One day she appeared at my door with a subpoena. She had sued for unemployment compensation, and I was being subpoenaed as a witness! She lost, but it cured me of ever hiring someone because she's pretty.

"She played the game right. She always dressed to emphasize her sensuality, and her little hand squeezes and other hints indicated a willingness to have an affair, but she had picked the wrong boss. Unfortunately for her, even then, young and inexperienced as I was, I was interested in performance and capability. There were a couple of other managers in the office who probably would have kept her around for years. Her mistake was in her interviewing technique. She was so interested in selling herself, she was so inwardly directed, that she neglected to assess me, her interviewer. Had she done a good job of interviewing, she could have concluded that she would have to be a capable secretary in order to keep her job. So she received a setback to her career. She went from a position she was capable of handling (clerk) to one she couldn't handle and, thus, found herself on the street within a couple of months out of work."

This is the risk anyone takes when they rely solely on sex to get a job. You must be able to make a quick and accurate evaluation of the interviewer.

◗ The offensive question

Women have another problem to deal with and it's probably the biggest irritant that faces both interviewees and interviewers. This is the offensive question.

The first thing you must determine is whether the interviewer has a good business reason for asking the question you feel is offensive. If you think he has none (like asking if you sleep with your boy or girl friend), then you should handle it in the manner discussed in chapter 6, "The Question and the Answer."

The problem with the offensive question is that more often than not it is not intended to be offensive. The perfect example of it, and perhaps the one that is asked most often is, "Have you completed your family?" or its corollary: "Do you plan on having any (more) children?" The question is rarely asked of single women. This is mystifying because it is certainly logical to assume that a single woman will eventually get married and probably have children. (The legality of this question is covered later in the chapter on discrimination. The problem is that, legal or not, it is often asked, and you must be prepared to handle it properly.)

Most women immediately react by thinking, "He doesn't ask men this question, so why is he asking me? It's discriminatory and demeaning." But you must realize that there is probably a good business reason (maybe it's not legitimate, but it **is** a good business reason) for asking. Put yourself in the place of an employer. You are interviewing to fill a vacancy, which is a responsible position. You have budgeted that this position will be filled by a person who will assume a large responsibility load; that person is needed every day. You have also budgeted that the person filling this position will be absent from the job for two weeks each year for vacation and probably an additional five days because of illness. So you are counting on the person to be on the job forty-nine weeks each year.

If you're interviewing a young married woman who has, let's assume, a two-year-old child, you may think, "Well, she's young and married and already has one child. If she gets pregnant, she'll probably have to miss several weeks while having her child. That's on top of her vacation and normal illnesses.

Who's going to fill in for her while she's off? Do I have to train someone just to be her stand-in while she has children?"

If you recognize this worry, you may not be able to answer him 👉 adequately, but you won't make the mistake of reacting with hostility — and that's the worst thing that you can do. Try to recognize that the question is not being asked to put you down or to discriminate against you but to voice a concern. Then you can meet it with a logical reply like, "Well, I do plan on having more children, but don't feel that it will require me to be absent from my work for such an extended period that it would affect the performance of my tasks."

Compare that answer with the answer many women give: "That's my personal decision and is not relevant to my ability to perform this job." This answer is offensive to the interviewer and violates a cardinal rule of interviewing: the interviewee must take care of the interviewer. To give this answer ignores a real concern of his and invites rejection.

One of your alternatives is to give this answer and then when you are rejected to file a discrimination complaint against the company. If that's your inclination, you'd better be prepared to become a professional plaintiff.

CHECKLIST

* Honestly assess what you have to offer.
* Recognize if your skills are so poor that your attractiveness is your best asset.
* Recognize the pitfalls of accepting an offer based upon sex or the promise of sex.
* If you accept a job based on sex appeal rather than skill, be prepared to change jobs often.
* Women should not react to genuine compliments with hostility.
* Evaluate the interviewer's motivation.
* If you feel a job is offered partly because of sex, but evaluate the interviewer as a professional and feel you can do a good job, don't turn the job down.

* If you don't respect the interviewer as a professional, you should be wary of accepting an offer based on sex.

* Treat requests for dates as an indication of the interviewer and what may happen after you accept a job.

* Men should anticipate questions about marital status.

* Determine whether the interviewer has a good business reason for asking a question that offends you and answer it accordingly.

* Don't be too sensitive or you'll never progress through the interview.

13

DECISIONS

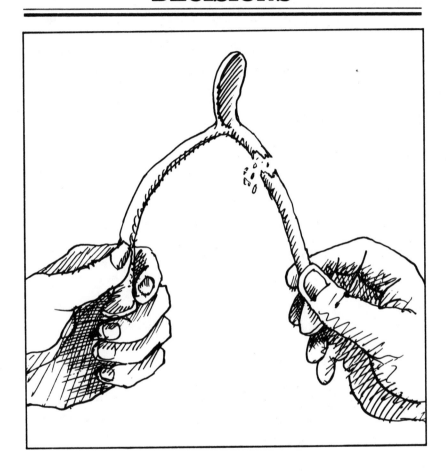

Although those who write about how to conduct interviews would have us believe that decisions are made empirically, the fact is that most decisions are made on visceral reactions to interviewees by the person making the decision. Sometimes this feeling is arrived at very quickly. Theodore Sorensen, who became President Kennedy's special counsel, was hired as a legislative assistant to the newly elected Senator Kennedy in 1953 after two five-minute interviews.

The "halo" effect, which Lopez (in *Personnel Interviewing Theory and Practice*) defines as "the undue influence of an irrelevant trait on [the interviewer's] overall judgment," is probably the dominant factor in making a selection decision. The consequence of the halo effect can be devastating. I once made a terrible error that epitomizes the halo effect. I had been interviewing for a long time to fill a position in the law department for a client corporation. I simply could not find the right person for the job.

Finally I interviewed a candidate who seemed right only because of a short answer to one of my questions. He was an assistant counsel in a corporation and I asked him what he did.

"I don't know," he replied. "I can't tell you specifics. All I know is that I'm always busy during the day and am always tired when I come home. I don't know why, but I just can't tell you specifically what I handle each day—but there are always a lot of people who have problems who want to see me and they always return with more problems."

I made up my mind to hire him then and there. Why? Because as a young lawyer working for Litton Industries, I had had the same problem. I was always terribly busy, people were always lining up at my door to see me, but when my friends asked me what I did, I couldn't tell them. He had expressed my feelings on the matter exactly.

Despite unanimous negative replies on my reference checks with his ex-employers, I hired him. It turned out that he had irreconcilable personality defects, which verified the reference checks. But the halo I put around his answer struck such a responsive chord in me that it superseded the empirical data I compiled of an unimpressive résumé and poor reference checks to such an extent that I offered him the job.

Lopez tells how an interviewer makes a decision. I offer his insights here with the caveat that he is talking of a screening interviewer who is a scientist in the interviewing process and not a selection interviewer. But the criteria he discusses may be relevant to both.

If the interview has been conducted properly, a great many imperfections and weaknesses will have been discovered in the applicant. If not, there was something wrong with the interview or the selection program. This unfavorable information can be quite misleading and can create a halo effect in reverse when compared to the man specification. . . .

The shrewd evaluator weighs a man's weaknesses against his strengths to arrive at an overall appraisal. . . . He employs a system of checks and balances, to determine what asset of the interviewee will compensate for what weakness. In any occupation, despite the allegations of some job analysts and methods engineers, there is no set pattern of requisite human attributes. Lack of formal education can be more than offset by an unusually varied and broad life experience; deficiencies in intellectual depth can be compensated for by an abundance of persistency, dedication and energy.

Some defects, of course, cannot be compensated for. A lack of ambition or drive can never be offset by a high level of intelligence or by a scintillating personality; job knowledge and skill cannot overcome personal maladjustment. To sum up, since an employee's success can be attributed to his own unique combination of personal characteristics, no job specification that merely lists a series of personal traits and the minimum requirement on each is sufficiently flexible to be adequate.

▶ Your past is prologue

One thing to realize is that the older you are and the more you've been around, the more you are inescapably wedded to your past. "What's past is prologue" is a rule that most selection interviewers follow. If the candidate has a history of personality conflicts with supervisors, the conclusion will be that this problem will not change. If the candidate has a history of missing a lot of work for sickness, this will be considered in evaluating his future performance. If he is late often, this will be considered.

You should be aware of any of these traits you possess. One of your objectives will be to establish a rapport with the interviewer so that he can accept these defects, either with a plausible explanation as to why they are not your norm or by convincing him that your assets—be they motivation, ambition, intelligence, personality, or leadership—far outweigh your track record of defects.

This is where your preparation will be most important. If you know yourself and you know that your defects will be revealed, you must prepare the interview so that you know how to downplay your defects and sell your assets. The more defects that you have that are revealed on your record, the more important it is that you control the interview so that the discussion is geared toward your strengths and away from your weaknesses.

Most decisions are made viscerally

How are decisions made? Selection decisions are no different from any other decision that we must all make. Much more often than not, decisions are made by choosing the path of least resistance. If you note the manner in which the following hundred million dollar decision was made, you'll be less impressed with the science involved in the decision-making process and less intimidated by how the decision on you is to be made.

In 1948 Henry Ford II first put forth the idea of bringing out a new car. It was not until 1955, however, after exhaustive studies, that Ford made the big decision and put their final approval on the project.

A team was formed, and millions of dollars were spent in research relating to the design and marketing of the new car. One of the fundamental decisions that had to be made was what to call it. Very early it was suggested that the car be named after Henry Ford II's father, Edsel, but Ford and his brothers quickly scotched that idea, saying that they didn't believe their father would "care to have his name spinning on a million hubcaps."

So several research consultants were hired and the entire nation was canvassed. People were asked their reactions to over two thousand names. Ford also consulted the poetess Marianne Moore, who suggested such zingers as Intelligent Bullet and Utopian Turtletop. They next went to Madison Avenue and their advertising agency, Foote, Cone & Belding, which came up with 18,000 possibilities in the twinkling of an eye (including Drof). They cut this list down to 6,000 and presented it to Ford. "There you are," an agency rep said proudly, "six thousand names, all alphabetized and cross-referenced."

"But," gasped a Ford executive, "we don't want six thousand names. We only want one." So Foote, Cone & Belding reduced the list of six thousand to ten and presented it to Ford's executive committee at a time when the three Ford brothers were away. The chairman of the committee looked at the ten suggestions and said, "I don't like any of them. Let's call it the Edsel." And that was that. After millions of dollars and months of research and work, the name chosen was the first one that had been suggested over a year earlier. It was also the only one to have been categorically rejected by the top person.

And you think that the hire-no hire decision on you is going to be made scientifically? Don't kid yourself. Most decisions, regardless of the amount of money riding on them, are made viscerally.

 ## Methods of reaching a decision

In *Principles of Selling,* H. K. Nixon gives five methods of reaching a decision.

1. **The method of logical reasoning.**
2. **The method of reason followed by voluntary decision.**
3. **The method of reason followed by emotional decision.**
4. **The method of reason followed by suggestion.**
5. **The method of suggestion.**

Most decisions are made by methods three and four. Emotion is the most important factor in decisions made by emotional people. No matter how much logic is used, no matter how reasonable the person making the decision, the deciding factor will almost invariably be based upon emotion, a feeling.

Ford, in making its decision to name the car the Edsel, rejected the advice of experts and made a final choice that was almost incomprehensible. They chose a name that had not been canvassed with the public, had no connotations of excitement or adventure (such as Corsair, which was the favored choice of Foote, Cone based upon their research), and had been rejected by the boss.

Why? The man who made the decision, the chairman, obviously reacted to some inner feeling he had about the other names and the one he chose. Could he define the feeling? Unlikely. Could he explain how he arrived at his decision? Doubtful. It was not arrived at through weighing empirical values. He looked at all the names and he had a feeling. "Let's call it the Edsel."

This is how you are going to be judged in your interview. The way an interviewer makes a decision on an applicant cannot be explained through logic. The interviewer will have some specific things for which he will be looking. And a candidate who does not measure up to this specification will be rejected. But the affirmative decision to make an offer will not be made simply because you fit the specification. There is something more. You must spark that feeling in him. If you do, you'll probably get an offer. If the interviewer is then asked why he made you an offer, he will most probably reply that you fit the specification for which he was looking. But that's not an accurate answer. Others fit the specification, too, But you hit that feeling and so you got the offer.

14

SALARY

There is perhaps no subject that worries an interviewee more than how to handle salary and benefits. For some reason candidates for jobs seem to feel that it is insulting to the employer to discuss salary. In fact, they often feel apologetic in telling the interviewer they expect to be paid for performing a service. There is no reason to feel apologetic, of course, but the subject of salary is something that you should handle very carefully.

▶ Don't bring it up yourself

☞ In the first place, it is the one subject that you should not bring up yourself. The interviewer, no matter how inexperienced, will not want to discuss salary with you until he has formed some sort of favorable opinion of you.

One reason is that he does not want anyone else to know what he may be willing to pay. You may be more qualified than another person he may interview. If he mentions a salary range to you that is higher than what he may be willing to pay another, he could be put in a difficult position if he made a lower offer to another who knows what he had quoted you.

Another reason is that he doesn't want to waste his time discussing something that is of interest solely to you before he knows something about you. If he decides he doesn't want to make you an offer, why should he waste his time discussing salary with you? After all, he knows what he is willing to pay. So if you broach the subject yourself before he has made a determination that he is interested in you, you run a very real risk of turning him off. Since one of your goals is to have the interviewer form a positive feeling about you, you don't want to risk offending him by asking about salary too early. Such a query can easily result in a negative inference that can ruin your chance for establishing the feeling requisite to your being considered further.

Leave the subject of salary for him to bring up. If, as the interview winds down, he says he wants to see you again or does something else to lead you to conclude that you are still being considered, then you can risk bringing it up yourself. The way to do it is to simply ask him what the position pays. Don't beat around the bush.

▶ Know yourself

The preparation I discussed earlier involves far more than doing research on the company and the person who is interviewing you. It entails looking inside yourself and coming to grips with who you are, what you want, and where you're going.

The best interviewee is the one who knows himself. If you 👉 are sure you know what you want and you express this in an interview, you must stick with it. To back down results in a negative impression and probably rejection.

Several years ago I was told a story by a young lawyer who had become confused by his recent interviewing experience. He had interviewed with the general counsel of a fairly large corporation, and when the subject of salary came up he told his interviewer that he would accept nothing less than $30,000. The interviewer told the candidate that this was beyond his budget. But he liked the man and tried to persuade him to accept $25,000. The candidate was firm. He wouldn't take anything less than $30,000. The general counsel accepted this statement. Impressed, he recommended the candidate to a friend of his, the general counsel of another corporation who was looking for an experienced attorney.

The candidate was interviewed by the second company, and both seemed to hit it off. When it came time to discuss salary, the candidate said that he wanted $30,000. The interviewer, a dynamic individual, told him that he couldn't go over $26,000.

Had the candidate been sophisticated, he would have recognized the $26,000 offer as a blatant ploy. Analyzing the situation objectively, he knew that he had been recommended to the second company by the general counsel who had made him an offer of $25,000, which he had adamantly turned down. At the time of rejecting the offer, he had made clear that his demand for $30,000 was not negotiable.

He knew that the first general counsel had recommended him to the second company and certainly could safely assume that his rejection of the $25,000 offer had been revealed and his demand for $30,000 made known.

He should have been able to draw the conclusion that the second company would be willing to pay him $30,000 or they would not have wasted their time interviewing him. They knew his salary demands before they interviewed him, and they had been given to understand that his demands were firm.

Why then the offer of $26,000? It could only have been a ploy, testing his conviction. Had they not been impressed with the interview, they would have made him no offer. Since they made him an offer, it is clear that they were prepared to pay him $30,000. The $26,000 offer was simply part of their interview technique to determine his character.

The candidate was inexperienced and had been swept off his feet by the interviewer. The first man he had interviewed had been low key and fairly quiet. The second man, on the other hand, was an outgoing fellow, and the candidate had been sold. He hesitated, then said that he was interested in the job and would like to think about it.

The next day the second interviewer called and told him that the offer was no longer open. Then the candidate called the first interviewer to see if he could accept his offer of $25,000 and was told that he was "too heavy" for the job.

From having two corporations pursuing him, he was down to zero. What had happened? Simple; he had come across very strongly that he knew his worth and was willing to walk away from any offer less than $30,000. This was impressive and earned him the respect of both men. When he showed interest at the lower figure, it was a sign of equivocation that caused both men to lose respect for him, resulting in rejection.

The sad part of this is that it was not equivocation or intent to deceive. The candidate wanted $30,000, but he was willing to accept a lower figure for the right job. His problem was that he didn't know this until it happened to him. He didn't know himself well enough, and this cost him two fine offers. Had he sat down beforehand and thought out his plan, he should have been able to determine the minimum he was willing to accept. Clearly his demand for $30,000 was a desire, not a requirement. But he had so little insight into himself that he thought that it was a requirement. When he discovered that he was willing to work for less, he had already presented himself as one with firm requirements and when he backed down, his integrity suffered. The conclusion drawn by his two interviewers was that he was less than candid when the fact was that he was just too immature to know himself.

Once you present something as a requirement, you cannot back down. Oscar-winning director of *It Happened One Night* and many other films, Frank Capra, tells of his first interview with Mack Sennett, the "king of comedy" in the 1920s, and it is a good example of setting a requirement and sticking with it.

Capra in the early 1920s had been writing "Our Gang" comedies for Hal Roach. But he wanted to be a director, so a friend arranged for an interview with Felix Adler, the head writer at Sennett's production company. After a short conversation with Adler, he was introduced to John Waldron, Sennett's accountant, who offered Capra $35 per week. Capra turned it down, saying that he got $40 at Roach.

Waldron wasn't impressed, saying that the rule was that beginners start at $35. Capra responded that he felt to take less than what he had been making would be going in the wrong direction and that he wanted to go toward the top.

Waldron icily replied that when one works for Sennett, he's **at** the top and that $35 was his only offer. Capra could take it or leave it.

Capra said, "I swallowed hard. 'Then I'll leave it, Mr. Waldron.' . . . My knees shook. I blew it. My big chance to work at Sennett's—and I blew it."

On the way out they stopped by Sennett's office. Waldron mentioned to Sennett that Capra wouldn't accept the beginner's $35 and that he wanted $45. Sennett asked Capra why he thought he was worth $45.

Capra said, "Mr. Sennett, what's the difference what you pay me? If you don't think I'm worth it you'll fire me in two minutes anyway."

Sennett said that it was $35 or nothing, that he wouldn't break any of his own rules.

Capra replied, "Mr. Sennett, I'm not asking you to break **any** rules. John Waldron starts me on the books at $35. Okay? Tomorrow you raise me to $45. Everybody's happy and no rules broken."

Capra got the job. He knew himself well enough to know that he would not take less than he had been making in his previous job. He was willing to walk away from a job he wanted desperately rather than compromise. He stuck to his guns and got what he wanted. Capra, unlike the candidate who changed his demands, would not have found the offer withdrawn had he accepted the $35. That's not the point of presenting his story here. The thing to note is that he was an intelligent, thoughtful man who knew himself well enough to know the difference between a requirement and a desire. Even though he felt that he had let an attractive job slip through his fingers, he was still willing to walk away from it. He knew he would not be happy with himself if he started a new job making less money than he had been making the previous week.

The first candidate discussed above had no such feeling. His $30,000 was a desire only. But when he discovered that he was willing to work for less, he had already planted himself in concrete, and when he changed his position, he destroyed the impression he had made that he was a confident man with integrity.

Don't paint yourself into a corner by trying a bluff you really don't believe in and are not willing to back all the way. If it's called and you back down, it may be too late.

 You must plan and prepare by looking deeply into yourself and deciding the parameters of what you **must** have and what you would like to have. If you don't get what you must have, you aren't losing anything by taking a firm stand. Since you can't back down, you are safe in taking a strong position.

In discussing points that you desire but can survive without, always leave yourself an escape so that you can give in without losing face. Determining the difference between your needs and your desires is an essential part of your preparation, and it requires an honest analysis of yourself.

How well do you know yourself? Do you remember what you've done in the past? That sounds pretty easy doesn't it? Of course you remember what you've done. Think so? How many times have you seen a long-lost friend and been reminded of an episode in your past of which you hadn't thought in years? Do you think you would have thought of that episode had your friend not jarred your memory?

Being interviewed consists in part of being deft in the conversational art. You are what you have done. In order to realize what you are, you must remember what you have done and be able to relate it. If you don't remember it, you won't be able to relate it. Further, you may misconstrue what you are.

▶ Write a diary

What Color Is Your Parachute is a job-seeking manual by Richard Nelson Bolles. In it, he advises job seekers to write their autobiography, what he calls the diary of their entire life. This is excellent advice. It requires dedication and a great deal of time, but it can help you gain insights into yourself.

To do it properly, it should be written chronologically. Start ☞ *at the beginning and go through each year, setting down incidents as they occurred. Don't be afraid to get help. If you remember someone from your past who participated in something with you but your memory is a little fuzzy, contact them for their recollections. This will not only help you in remembering what happened, it may trigger other memories.*

This can run into hundreds of pages and tens of thousands of words, but when you're done, you'll have a compendium of your experiences. You can use it to make a good assessment of who you are and what you have to offer, and it will be a ready reference of things about which you may wish to speak to an interviewer. Additionally, and maybe even more importantly, it may trigger clues about things you wish to avoid discussing with an interviewer.

Once you have your story down on paper, you have to come to grips with two things: what you want and what you have to offer. What you want can be subdivided into how much money you want and what kind of work you want.

▶ How much money you need

How much money you need and how much you desire are two ☞ *completely different things.*

You can determine how much you need by preparing a simple budget. How much does it cost you to live? Write down your rent or mortgage payment, how much you spend on food each month, what your car payments are, how much you spend on clothes, utilities, gasoline, cleaning, and so forth. Then check this with your monthly bank reconciliations for the past year. You may find that your memory is faulty and you're spending more than you realize. In any event, know exactly how much you have to earn in order to live. This is your basic salary requirement. You may **desire** more money (don't we all?)

but you can live on this amount. So if worse comes to worse and a job offer is made for a job you would enjoy and it meets this amount, you can take it without feeling that you are making a financial mistake.

▶ What will make you happy

The second element you must analyze is what you want to do. What kind of a job will make you happy? Only you can answer this. Some people are happy if they spend the entire day typing. That would drive others up a wall. Some are happy selling brushes door to door. Others would drink themselves into a stupor if they had to do that. Some are happy if they have a lot of responsibility. Others want to avoid responsibility.

One of the best ways to determine the elements of a job you want is to write two lists: one consisting of the things you enjoy in a job and the other consisting of the things you don't enjoy. Make this list as complete as possible. You won't be able to do this in one sitting. You may remember something while you're doing your marketing or are watching a baseball game. Whenever you think of a new element for one of the lists, write it down immediately; otherwise you may forget it. Then it'll not only be gone, but it can drive you crazy trying to remember it.

Once you have this list fairly complete, you should have a good job specification in terms of salary and function. It will give you a list of questions you know you will want to ask your interviewer. It will also give you the confidence that the interview is a two-way street; both you and the interviewer are interviewing each other.

▶ Desires versus requirements

Finally, divide the list containing the elements you enjoy in a job into two categories, one containing the items you must have and the other containing the items you'd like but don't need. This is essential because the odds are that you're not going to find a job that contains everything you want.

You may find a good position but it's on the fortieth floor and you hate elevators, or it's next to a chain smoker and you're allergic to cigarette smoke, or it's located in Kansas and you love the ocean. Before you go into your interview, know the things that you must have and those that you can do without in a pinch. Maybe you can forgo seeing the ocean or can overcome your fear of elevators. Maybe you can't. If you can't, know it going in. But don't get yourself in a position of turning down the job in Kansas and later regretting it, realizing that the job was more important to you than the ocean.

Your list of requirements should be short. If it's not, you are going to find yourself in the job market for a long, long time because most jobs fall short of being ideal.

▶ Ensure that your wants are logical

During a counseling session I had with a job applicant, we took a break for lunch, and he drove me to a restaurant on the beach. He drove a truck, something unusual for an attorney, and en route I asked him why. "Money doesn't mean anything to me," he replied. "I don't have to work so I just do what I want. As a result I can't afford a big car so I drive this truck."

During lunch our counseling session continued, and he revealed that he had just been offered a job with great opportunity but had turned it down. When I asked why, he said that they were offering him only $27,500 and he felt he was "worth more than that."

I asked him how much he made at his last job, and he said $23,000. He was currently making less than $20,000. The reason he felt that he was worth more was because his friends all earned more than that. This is how many people judge their worth, but it's completely irrelevant unless the friends all have the same background, education, training, and experience. Here was a man who had never made more than $23,000 in his life turning down an attractive job offer for 20 percent more than he had ever made because it wasn't enough money.

Had I been interviewing him for a job, I probably would have dropped him right there. First he told me he didn't care about money, and then he said he turned down an attractive position solely because of money—an inherent inconsistency. Second, he had a grossly inflated value of himself based upon a false syllogism: My friends make more than $27,500; they are my friends; therefore I am worth more than $27,500.

The error of this reasoning is apparent. But it was not his faulty reasoning that would have spelled the coup de grace for him with me. It was the inconsistency in his telling me how he disdained money, yet the sole reason he had for rejecting a fine offer was money.

☞ You have a right to expect to be paid a reasonable salary and benefits in return for your work, and you shouldn't be shy about discussing them frankly and openly. But you must be pragmatic about what you want and what you feel you are worth. Don't worry about what your friends are making. That's irrelevant to what you should earn. Determine what **you** need, what **you** want, and what **you'll** settle for and know these three figures going in to the interview.

▶ When he asks how much you're making

One of the roughest problems faced by any interviewee comes when the interviewer asks how much the interviewee is making. Generally you are not making as much as you want to make or as much as you want your interviewer to offer you.

☞ As a general rule of thumb, someone who changes jobs wants an increase in salary of at least 20 percent. But what if you feel you are grossly underpaid and you want a much larger increase? What do you do when you are asked how much you are making?

It's a sad fact that employers will base their compensation more on what a candidate is making at his present job than on what the candidate is worth. If, for example, he has budgeted the job at $30,000 or $40,000 a year, and he finds that you are making $18,000 a year, it's unlikely that he'll offer you more than $22,000 even though he was originally willing to pay a lot more. Why? He knows he's in a buyer's market and your alternative is to stay where you are and continue making $18,000.

He's not about to offer you a 50 percent increase when he can probably get you for a 20 percent increase.

So what do you do when he asks what you're making?

*What you do **not** do is lie. You always run the risk of his* *verifying what you tell him. If you tell him you're making more than you actually are and he asks you for a W-2 or tax return or payroll stub, what can you say? If you refuse he'll assume that you were lying and will probably reject you on that basis alone.*

An exception is that you can always refuse to supply a copy of your tax return when an interviewer requests it. Simply tell him that you never reveal such private and confidential information to anyone. He has no right to ask for such a legal document, and you have no obligation to supply it. The problem is that if he wants it to verify what you've told him, he'll ask for some other type of verification, and you can't logically refuse a request he might make to have your present employer supply the verification.

You do have one ploy you can try if he asks you for salary information before discussing what he is willing to pay for the position. Before replying, you can ask what the position pays. This turns the tables on him. If he asks for salary information, it's an indication that he is interested in you and that he is planning on discussing salary with you.

The problem with this query is that you risk being offensive. But if you are earning a very low salary in relation to what you want and what you think he's willing to pay, you've got to try something that will deflect him from his course of finding out your salary. It's possible that this query will permanently keep him off the subject, but it's not likely.

The advantage is that if he is broaching salary by asking how much you make, he's indicating that he's interested. You must try and get him to reveal a salary range before you reveal how much you're making. If he tells you the range before you tell him that you make much less than that, it would be difficult and awkward for him to offer you less than the range he reveals. If you tell him your salary before he reveals the range,

when he does indicate the range it'll be a lot lower than it was
before you revealed your salary.

 *So the one rule to remember if you have a very low salary is
to try and get him to tell you the salary range of the position
for which you're interviewing* **before** *you tell him how much
you're making.*

▶ Vacation

Don't worry about asking about vacation. Employers do not
expect their employees to work fifty-two weeks a year (they
may want them to, but they don't expect it). Vacation is one of
the most important elements of a job, and you should not
shrink from asking about it. Most of the interviewers with
whom I have spoken expect—and welcome—questions about
vacation. You will not be jeopardizing your receiving further
consideration by letting the interviewer know that you are interested in the vacation and other job benefits. It's much better
for you to ask about it before you receive an offer. Where are
you if you take a job and then find out that you only get one
day off a year? If you knew that before, it would probably have
kept you from accepting an offer.

R. E. Taylor, vice-president of personnel administration for
the Bank of America, states a typical view: "It's not a negative
to ask about vacation. It's our experience that it's very important to people today. When I applied for a job, I just wanted a
job. We find that people's expectations are greater and more
varied than they were. Leisure time is important to them.
They're concerned about the environment and where they
want to live and work. It's very important to them. We have
people asking, 'Can I work downtown in the Towers? Can I
work by the beach?' I don't think we can afford to have that
type of question be a turnoff."

 *The general rule relating to vacation and benefits is that, like
salary, they are items you should not bring up until the interviewer has raised the subject or has let you know that he is
definitely interested in you. Once you have determined that,*

you should find out as much about the job–what it pays and what the responsibilities and benefits are–as you can.

CHECKLIST

★ Don't bring up the subject of salary yourself.

★ The interviewer won't want to discuss salary until he has made an initial determination that he is interested in you.

★ If it appears that the interview is ending with his expressing interest in seeing you again, then you can ask about salary.

★ If you raise the subject yourself, don't beat around the bush.

★ You must do research into yourself before you go into the interview.

★ Make a budget to determine how much money you must have.

★ Write a diary of your life.

★ Make a list of what things in a job will make you happy.

★ Make a list of the things in a job that you don't like.

★ Separate the list of what you like into requirements versus desires.

★ Ensure that your thinking is logical when you deal with your requirements.

★ Don't worry about what your friends are making.

★ Make a list of the things you have to offer an employer.

★ Try to find out what the job pays before you reveal your current salary.

★ Don't give the interviewer a copy of your tax return.

★ After he has revealed his interest in you, ask about vacation and benefits.

15

DISCRIMINATION

$\mathbf{T}$he law relating to what may and may not be asked during an interview is simple. Questions may not be asked for the purpose of discriminating on the basis of race, color, religion, sex, national origin, or age.

▶ Federal laws

Federal laws don't expressly prohibit an interviewer from asking questions about your race, color, religion, or national origin, but the Equal Employment Opportunity Commission (EEOC) has issued a statement that it regards such inquiries with "extreme disfavor." It also says:

Except in those infrequent instances where religion or national origin is a bona fide occupational qualification reasonably necessary for the performance of a particular job, an applicant's race, religion and the like are totally irrelevant to his or her ability or qualifications as a prospective employee, and no useful purpose is served by eliciting such information. . . .

Accordingly, in the investigation of charges alleging the commission of unlawful employment practices the Commission will pay particular attention to the use by the party against whom charges have been made of pre-employment inquiries concerning race, religion, color or national origin, or other inquiries which tend directly or indirectly to disclose such information. The fact that such questions are asked may, unless otherwise explained, constitute evidence of discrimination, and will weigh significantly in the Commission's decision as to whether or not [the law] has been violated.

State laws

State laws on the subject are more specific. Each state has laws relating to employment practices. They are generally known as fair employment practices laws and forbid employment bias based on race, color, sex, age, religion, national origin, or ancestry.

Basically what you need to remember is that a question *should be job related. The United States Supreme Court has said that "the touchstone is business necessity."*

Unlawful questions

Most states have lists of questions on subjects that they consider lawful and unlawful. Following are the California and New York lists. As you can see, they are similar. If you're familiar with these, you'll have a general feel for what's appropriate and what isn't. For your state's list, contact the Fair Employment Practices Commission in your state. It may not be called that in each state (in New York, for instance, it's called the State Division of Human Rights), but a phone call to your state office building will guide you to the right office. If you have a problem or a question, don't hesitate to call your state office or the EEOC. If you believe you've been discriminated against on the basis of age or handicap, you should contact the U.S. Department of Labor. They are there to serve you and can be very helpful.

 ## California

Lawful Pre-employment Inquiries	Subject	Unlawful Pre-employment Inquiries
"Have you worked for this company under a different name?" "Have you ever been convicted of a crime under another name?"	Name:	Former name of applicant whose name has been changed by court order or otherwise.*
Applicant's place of residence. How long applicant has been resident of this State or city.	Address or Duration of Residence:	
"Can you, after employment, submit a birth certificate or other proof of U. S. citizenship or age?"	Birthplace:	Birthplace of applicant. Birthplace of applicant's parents, spouse or other relatives. Requirement that applicant submit birth certificate, naturalization or baptismal record.†
"Can you, after employment, submit a work permit if under eighteen?" "Are you over eighteen years of age?" "If hired, can you furnish proof of age?" /or/Statement that hire is subject to verification that applicant's age meets legal requirements.	Age:	Questions which tend to identify applicants 40 to 64 years of age.
	Religious:	Applicant's religious denomination or affiliation, church, parish, pastor, or religious holidays observed. "Do you attend religious services /or/ a house of worship?" Applicant may not be told "This is a Catholic/Protestant/Jewish/atheist organization."
Statement by employer of regular days, hours or shift to be worked.	Work Days and Shifts:	
	Race or Color:	Complexion, color of skin, or other questions directly or indirectly indicating race or color.
Statement that photograph may be required after employment.	Photograph:	Requirement that applicant affix a photograph to his application form. Request applicant, at his option, to submit photograph. Requirement of photograph after interview but before hiring.†

Lawful Pre-employment Inquiries	Subject	Unlawful Pre-employment Inquiries
"If you are not a U. S. citizen, have you the legal right to remain permanently in the U. S.? Do you intend to remain permanently in the U. S.?" Statement by employer that if hired, applicant may be required to submit proof of citizenship.	Citizenship:	"Are you a citizen of the United States?" Whether applicant or his parents or spouse are naturalized or native-born United States citizens. Date when applicant or parents or spouse acquired U. S. citizenship. Requirement that applicant produce his naturalization papers or first papers.† Whether applicant's parents or spouse are citizens of the U. S.
Languages applicant reads, speaks or writes fluently.	National Origin or Ancestry:	Applicant's nationality, lineage, ancestry, national origin, descent or parentage. Date of arrival in United States or port of entry; how long a resident. Nationality of applicant's parents or spouse; maiden name of applicant's wife or mother. "Language commonly used by applicant/ what is your mother tongue?" How applicant acquired ability to read, write or speak a foreign language.
Applicant's academic, vocational, or professional education; schools attended.	Education:	Date last attended high school.
Applicant's work experience. Applicant's military experience in armed forces of United States, in a state militia (U. S.), or in a particular branch of U. S. armed forces.	Experience:	Applicant's military experience (general) Type of military discharge.
"Have you ever been convicted of any crime?" If so, when, where, and disposition of case?	Character:	"Have you ever been arrested?"
Names of applicant's relatives already employed by this company. Name and address of parent or guardian if applicant is a minor.	Relatives	Marital status or number of dependents. Name or address of relative, spouse or children of adult applicant. "With whom do you reside?" "Do you live with your parents?"
Name and address of person to be notified in case of accident or emergency.	Notice in Case of Emergency:	Name and address of relative to be notified in case of accident or emergency.
Organizations, clubs, professional societies, or other associations of which applicant is a member excluding any the names or character of which indicates the race, religious creed, color, national origin, or ancestry of its members.	Organizations:	"List all organizations, clubs, societies, and lodges to which you belong."
"By whom were you referred for a position here?"	References:	Requirement of submission of a religious reference.
"Do you have any physical condition which may limit your ability to perform the job applied for?" Statement by employer that offer may be made contingent on passing a physical examination.	Physical Condition	"Do you have any physical disabilities?" Questions on general medical condition. Inquiries as to receipt of Workers' Compensation.
Notice to applicant that any misstatements or omissions of material facts in his application may be cause for dismissal.	Miscellaneous	Any inquiry that is not job-related or necessary for determining an applicant's eligibility for employment.

Notes:

* The employer may ask other names under which the applicant has worked (for example, a married woman applicant's maiden name), if he must have such names in order to check the educational or employment records or references, and if it is his standard practice to check such references.

† Documents such as birth certificates or naturalization papers, which reveal race and birthplace, and often religion, may not be required prior to hiring; likewise, photographs or any evidence of race, religion, or national origin. The Commission has ruled that the point of hire is reached once the employer has decided to hire the applicant and has so informed him. When this point has been reached, the otherwise forbidden inquiries may be made. Thus any proof needed to support claims made by the applicant —e. g., as to U. S. citizenship, veteran status, age—may be inspected by the employer before the individual actually goes on the payroll. If the proof is lacking, the hire need not be consummated.

 # New York

Directly Revelatory Inquiries

The Law expressly prohibits employers, employment agencies, landlords, and real estate sellers, brokers and salespersons, and creditors from asking certain questions either in an application form or in a personal interview *before* selecting an employee, apprentice or tenant or making a real estate sale or lease, or extending credit. The following are examples of different types of inquiries that have been ruled lawful or unlawful:

Subject	Lawful *	Unlawful
Race or Color:		Complexion or color of skin. Coloring.
Religion or Creed:		Inquiry into applicant's religious denomination, religious affiliations, church, parish, pastor or religious holidays observed. Applicant may not be told "This is a (Catholic, Protestant, or Jewish) organization."
National Origin:		Inquiry into applicant's lineage, ancestry, national origin, descent, parentage or nationality. Nationality of applicant's parents or spouse. What is your mother tongue?
Sex:		Inquiry as to sex. Do you wish to be addressed as Mr.? Mrs.? Miss? or Ms.?
Marital Status:		Are you married? Are you single? Divorced? Separated? Name or other information about spouse. Where does your spouse work? What are the ages of your children, if any?
Birth Control:		Inquiry as to capacity to reproduce, advocacy of any form of birth control or family planning.

* Inquiries which would otherwise be deemed lawful may, in certain circumstances, be deemed as evidence of unlawful discrimination when the inquiry seeks to elicit information about a selection criterion which is not job-related and which has a disproportionately burdensome effect upon the members of a minority group and cannot be justified by business necessity.

Subject	Lawful	Unlawful
Age:	Are you between 18 and 65 years of age? If not, state your age.	How old are you? What is your date of birth?
Disability:	Do you have any impairments, physical, mental, or medical, which would interfere with your ability to perform the job for which you have applied? If there are any positions or types of positions for which you should not be considered, or job duties you cannot perform because of a physical, mental or medical disability, please describe.	Do you have a disability? Have you ever been treated for any of the following diseases . . . ?
Arrest Record:	Have you ever been convicted of a crime? (Give details.)**	Have you ever been arrested?

It is unlawful to ask questions the answers to which will indirectly reveal information as to race, creed, color, national origin, sex, marital status, disability, age or arrest record in cases where such information may not be asked directly. The same exceptions apply. In making such rulings, the Division has applied a rule of reason, taking into account the need for the information asked as well as the danger that it will reveal other information that should not be considered in selection.

The following are Division rulings on inquiries indirectly revelatory of race, creed, color, national origin, sex, marital status, disability, age or arrest record:

Subject	Lawful	Unlawful
Name:	Have you ever worked for this company under a different name? Is any additional information relative to change of name, use of an assumed name or nickname necessary to enable a check on your work record? If yes, explain.	Original name of an applicant whose name has been changed by court order or otherwise. Maiden name of a married woman. If you have ever worked under another name, state name and dates.
Address or Duration of Residence:	Applicant's place of residence. How long a resident of this state or city?	
Birthplace:		Birthplace of applicant. Birthplace of applicant's parents, spouse or other close relatives.
Birthdate:		Requirement that applicant submit birth certificate, naturalization or baptismal record. Requirement that applicant produce proof of age in the form of a birth certificate or baptismal record.
Photograph:		Requirement or option that applicant affix a photograph to employment form at any time before hiring.

** Effective January 1, 1977, an applicant may not be denied employment because of a conviction record unless there is a direct relationship between the offense and the job or unless hiring would be an unreasonable risk. An ex-offender denied employment is entitled to a statement of the reasons for such denial. Correction Law, Article 23-A, § 754.

Subject	Lawful	Unlawful
Citizenship:	Are you a citizen of the United States?	Of what country are you a citizen?
	If not a citizen of the United States, do you intend to become a citizen of the United States? If you are not a United States citizen, have you the legal right to remain permanently in the United States? Do you intend to remain permanently in the United States?	Whether an applicant is naturalized or a native-born citizen; the date when the applicant acquired citizenship.
		Requirement that applicant produce naturalization papers or first papers.
	Requirement that applicant state whether he or she has ever been interned or arrested as an enemy alien.	Whether applicant's parents or spouse are naturalized or native-born citizens of the United States; the date when such parents or spouse acquired citizenship.
Language:	Inquiry into languages applicant speaks and writes fluently.	What is your native language?
		Inquiry into how applicant acquired ability to read, write or speak a foreign language.
Education:	Inquiry into applicant's academic, vocational or professional education and the public and private schools attended.	
Experience:	Inquiry into work experience.	
Relatives:	Names of applicant's relatives, other than a spouse, already employed by this company.	Names, addresses, ages, number or other information concerning applicant's spouse, children or other relatives not employed by the company.
Notice in Case of Emergency:	Name and address of person to be notified in case of accident or emergency.	
Military Experience:	Inquiry into applicant's military experience in the Armed Forces of the United States or in a State Militia.	Inquiry into applicant's general military experience.
	Inquiry into applicant's service in particular branch of United States Army, Navy, etc.	
Organizations:	Inquiry into applicant's membership in organizations which the applicant considers relevant to his or her ability to perform the job.	List all clubs, societies and lodges to which you belong.

▶ How to respond to an unlawful question

What do you do if someone asks you an unlawful question, for example, whether you have ever been arrested? If you don't answer it, the interviewer may think that you are hiding something. If you call him on it, you'll either offend him or scare him or both. In any event, you run a great risk of blowing the interview, leaving you only with the option of filing a discrimination claim against him—and that's not as good as getting an offer.

If your reply can't hurt you, you should answer the question but let the interviewer know that you know the law. For the question about arrests, a good answer would be, "Well, I've never been arrested, but didn't I read somewhere that that's not an appropriate question to ask in an interview?" Try and say this ingenuously, not in an accusing or threatening tone. It should warn him that you know what he cannot ask, and you haven't offended him.

If, however, the question probes an area where you might be hurt, you should not answer it. Again, decline in a manner that does not pose a threat to him.

Don't say, "That's against the law for you to ask me that." You can decline in a much better way. You can turn the tables on him by asking facetiously, "Why? Do I look like an ex-con?" and then laugh. If he then persists, you can say, "I thought you were kidding because I thought everyone knew that that is the classic pre-employment inquiry that is a no-no. You don't really want to ask me that, do you?"

Then you've got him. If he persists, you've set him up for a discrimination charge. If he drops it, he's still going to have to worry about your filing a discrimination charge against him if he doesn't make you an offer. But you haven't threatened him, nor have you given him the impression that you're litigious.

You can use the second part of the answer suggested above no matter what prohibited inquiry he asks. The first part must be tailored to the question. But if you don't want to answer it, you are better off treating it as if he's kidding (even though you know he's not) and then turn the tables on him if he persists in seeking an answer.

Another possible answer causes problems. You could say, "I'm willing to cooperate with you in your legitimate areas of inquiry, but it's my understanding that questions that are not job related are inappropriate. I don't think whether I've ever been arrested or whether I'm married or whether I'm religious are relevant to the job for which I'm interviewing. Do you?" But then you risk embarrassing the interviewer and destroying any positive feeling he may have developed. Other than that, it's a good answer in that you're not zeroing in on just the specific unlawful question asked. By broadening the answer to include other areas of prohibited inquiry, you take from the interviewer the thought that you aren't answering because the answer may hurt you.

▶ Purpose of question

If a prohibited question is asked and you don't get an offer, it doesn't follow that you have a claim. **The question must have been asked for the purpose of discriminating against you because of an illegal reason or have the effect of discriminating against you.** This may not be easy to determine, although an interviewer who has asked such a question may have difficulty explaining why he asked it if not to make a hire-no hire decision based upon your answer.

▶ Filing periods

If you feel that you were asked a prohibited pre-employment inquiry and, as a result, were discriminated against, you should file a charge within 180 days. You should file concurrently with both your state agency and the EEOC. The filing periods in the various states vary with state law, so you should call your state agency to ensure what the filing period is (the federal period for the EEOC is 180 days). As a matter of procedure, the EEOC will defer until the state agency has investigated and taken action; then the EEOC will investigate after the state agency deferral has ended.

After the EEOC conducts an investigation, it will make a determination to see if there is reasonable cause to believe that your charge is true. Although the EEOC is making an effort to reduce its backlog of charges, it currently may take years to institute an investigation. If you wish to proceed against the employer sooner, you may request a notice to sue 180 days after you file your charge with the EEOC. If the EEOC investigates, you will not take part in the investigation, and you do not need an attorney. All of the EEOC's investigation is confidential. All you'll find out is whether the EEOC has determined if there is reasonable cause to believe your charge is true. If the EEOC does not find such reasonable cause, it will advise you of this and of your "right to sue" in court.

▶ Conciliation

If the EEOC does find reasonable cause, it will attempt to conciliate the matter by meeting with the potential employer and reaching an agreement on the remedy. If no agreement is reached, the EEOC may file a suit or it may issue you a "right to sue" letter. You have 90 days after receipt of a "right to sue" letter from the EEOC to file your own suit.

▶ Attorneys

If you don't have an attorney, the courts are authorized to appoint one for you and to start the action without payment of a filing fee. Just because the EEOC does not find reasonable cause does not mean that you can't file a suit yourself, and it doesn't mean that you won't recover.

▶ Filing the lawsuit yourself

If you can afford an attorney, you should retain your own. But if you can't, it has been held that all you have to do is file your "right to sue" letter in federal court and apply for the appointment of counsel. If you do these things within the 90-day period after receipt of your "right to sue" letter, you should be safe in having preserved your cause of action.

▶ Remedies

The remedies you can hope to receive if you get a favorable judgment from the court can include attorney's fees. So if you retain your own attorney and win, the employer may have to pay your attorney. Of course you can also get damages. For example, perhaps you can prove that you were not hired because of discrimination. If the job for which you were interviewing paid $20,000 per year and you were out of work for a year thereafter and couldn't get a job despite diligent effort, the court could award you $20,000 in damages.

▶ State and local governments are liable

State and local governments are **not** immune from paying salary and attorneys' fees in cases of prohibited discrimination.

Although you may be awarded your attorneys' fees if you win, you might have to pay the other party's attorneys' fees if you lose. Although this is very rare, it has happened and it is something of which you should be aware.

▶ Put the law in context

Now that you have a general idea of what your rights are if you are asked a prohibited pre-employment inquiry, you must put this knowledge in the context of everything you've learned in this book. The one thing to remember is that the inquiry must have been asked for the purpose of discriminating against you for an unlawful reason.

One point that has been hammered away in this book is that **most** selection interviewers are **unsophisticated.** They don't ask predetermined questions. They will ask you whatever pops into their heads. So they may ask you if you're religious because **they** are religious and wonder if you go to the same church or temple. In this event, it would have nothing to do with whether they're going to hire you. Or you may be asked the derivation of your name because the interviewer thinks you're nervous and this would be something you could talk about freely to relieve the tension, rather than finding out if you really are Estonian because the interviewer hates all Estonians.

An interview is a place where the interviewer is trying to find out what kind of a person you are and whether he has a good feeling about you. If you really think that he's trying to find out prohibited things for the purpose of discriminating and you don't get an offer you want, then you should feel free to file a claim with the state and the EEOC. But think about it and be sure that you really feel in your heart that you were discriminated against. Don't just file a charge on a whim or out of pique because you didn't get an offer.

CHECKLIST

★ Pre-employment inquiries may not be asked for the purpose of discriminating on the basis of race, color, religion, sex, national origin, or age.

★ The Equal Employment Opportunity Commission views such inquiries with "extreme disfavor."

★ State laws specifically prohibit bias.

★ Most states have lists of lawful and unlawful questions.

★ The first time you're asked an unlawful question, answer it if your reply can't hurt you, and then let the interviewer know that you know what may and may not be asked during an interview.

★ If the answer will hurt you, treat the question facetiously while declining to answer.

★ If the interviewer persists, tell him you thought he was kidding because "everyone knows" the inquiry is prohibited.

★ You don't have a claim unless the purpose of the question was to discriminate for an unlawful reason.

★ At present your initial filing period is 180 days after the prohibited question is asked.

★ You should file with both the state and the EEOC.

★ You may not file a lawsuit in court until you have received a "right to sue" letter from the EEOC.

★ You can file a suit in court by filing your "right to sue" letter along with an application for appointment of counsel.

★ Your remedies include damages and attorneys' fees.

★ State and local governmental employers are not immune from being ordered to pay damages because of illegal discrimination.

★ You may have to pay the other party's attorneys' fees if you lose.

★ Don't file a claim unless you are certain the question was asked for the purpose of discriminating against you.

Appendix A

COMMONLY ASKED QUESTIONS

This appendix consists of three sections of questions commonly asked in the selection interview. The first section contains questions reported by ninety-two companies surveyed by *The Northwestern Endicott Report*, published and copyrighted by the Placement Center, Northwestern University. Although they are aimed at student interviews, many of the questions are asked when interviewing candidates of all ages.

The second section contains questions suggested by Walter R. Mahler in his book *How Effective Executives Interview*. Questions in this section usually are used when interviewing people already in the job market.

The third section sets forth additional questions that can pop up in an interview and for which an interviewee should be prepared.

You can expect to be asked some of the questions in this appendix in an interview. I suggest that you go through a mock interview and have these questions shot at you. If you are prepared for these, it's unlikely that you'll be caught unaware in the actual interview.

▶ Section 1

1. What are your future vocational plans?
2. In what school activities have you participated? Why? Which did you enjoy the most?
3. How do you spend your spare time? What are your hobbies?
4. In what type of position are you most interested?
5. Why do you think you might like to work for our company?
6. What jobs have you held? How were they obtained, and why did you leave?
7. What courses did you like best? Least? Why?
8. Why did you choose your particular field of work?

9. What percentage of your college expenses did you earn? How?
10. How did you spend your vacations while in school?
11. What do you know about our company?
12. Do you feel that you have received a good general training?
13. What qualifications do you have that make you feel that you will be successful in your field?
14. What extracurricular offices have you held?
15. What are your ideas on salary?
16. How do you feel about your family?
17. How interested are you in sports?
18. If you were starting college all over again, what courses would you take?
19. Can you forget your education and start from scratch?
20. Do you prefer any specific geographic location? Why?
21. Do you have a girl (boy) friend? Is it serious?
22. How much money do you hope to earn at age ————?
23. Why did you decide to go to the college you attended?
24. How did you rank in your graduating class in high school? College? Graduate school?
25. Do you think that your extracurricular activities were worth the time you devoted to them? Why?
26. What do you think determines a person's progress in a good company?
27. What personal characteristics are necessary for success in your chosen field?
28. Why do you think you would like this particular type of job?
29. What is your father's occupation?
30. Tell me about your home life during the time you were growing up.
31. Are you looking for a permanent or temporary job?
32. Do you prefer working with others or by yourself?
33. Who are your best friends?
34. What kind of boss do you prefer?
35. Are you primarily interested in making money, or do you feel that service to your fellow men is a satisfactory accomplishment?
36. Can you take instructions without feeling upset?
37. Tell me a story!
38. Do you live with your parents? Which of your parents has had the most profound influence on you?
39. How did previous employers treat you?
40. What have you learned from some of the jobs you have held?
41. Can you get recommendations from previous employers?
42. What interests you about our product or service?
43. What was your record in military service?

44. Have you ever changed your major field of interest? Why?
45. When did you choose your college major?
46. How did your college grades after military service compare with those previously earned?
47. Do you feel you have done the best work of which you are capable?
48. How did you happen to go to college?
49. What do you know about opportunities in the field in which you are trained?
50. How long do you expect to work?
51. Have you ever had any difficulty getting along with fellow students and faculty? Fellow workers?
52. Which of your college years was most difficult?
53. What is the source of your spending money?
54. Do you own any life insurance?
55. Have you saved any money?
56. Do you have any debts?
57. How old were you when you became self-supporting?
58. Do you attend church?
59. Did you enjoy college?
60. Do you like routine work?
61. Do you like regular work?
62. What size city do you prefer?
63. When did you first contribute to family income?
64. What is your major weakness?
65. Define cooperation.
66. Will you fight to get ahead?
67. Do you demand attention?
68. Do you have an analytical mind?
69. Are you eager to please?
70. What do you do to keep in good physical condition?
71. How do you usually spend Sunday?
72. Have you had any serious illness or injury?
73. Are you willing to go where the company sends you?
74. What job in our company would you choose if you were entirely free to do so?
75. Is it an effort for you to be tolerant of persons with a background and interests different from your own?
76. What types of books have you read?
77. Have you plans for further education?
78. What types of people seem to rub you the wrong way?
79. Do you enjoy sports as a participant? As an observer?
80. Have you ever tutored another student?
81. What jobs have you enjoyed the most? The least? Why?

82. What are your own special abilities?
83. What job in our company do you want to work toward?
84. Would you prefer a large or a small company? Why?
85. What is your idea of how industry operates today?
86. Do you like to travel?
87. How about overtime work?
88. What kind of work interests you?
89. What are the disadvantages of your chosen field?
90. Do you think that grades should be considered by employers? Why or why not?
91. Are you interested in research?
92. If married, how often do you entertain at home?
93. To what extent do you use liquor?
94. What have you done that shows initiative and willingness to work?

▶ Section II

1. Beginning with your move into your first supervisory job, would you tell me briefly why each change was made.
2. Referring to your most recent position, what would you say are some of your more important accomplishments? I'd be interested in operating results and any other accomplishments you consider important. (Probe for four or five accomplishments. Get specific data.)
3. Considering these accomplishments, what are some of the reasons for your success?
4. Were there any unusual difficulties you had to overcome in getting these accomplishments?
5. What two or three things do you feel you have learned on this job?
6. What did you particularly like about the position?
7. There are always a few negatives about a position. What would you say you liked least about the position?
8. What responsibilities or results have not come up to your expectations? I'd be interested in things you had hoped and planned to accomplish which were not done. I sometimes call them disappointments. (Push for several specific answers)
9. What are some of the reasons for this?
10. I'm interested in how you do your planning. What planning processes have you found useful, and how do you go about them?
11. In what way do you feel you have improved in your planning in the last few years?

12. What are some examples of important types of decisions or recommendations you are called upon to make?
13. Would you describe how you went about making these types of decisions or recommendations? With whom did you talk, and so forth?
14. What decisions are easiest for you to make and which ones are more difficult?
15. Most of us can think of an important decision which we would make quite differently if we made it again. Any examples from your experience? Probe: What's the biggest mistake you can recall?
16. Most of us improve in our decision-making ability as we get greater experience. In what respects do you feel you have improved in your decision making?
17. What has been your experience with major expansion or reduction of force? (Explore for details.)
18. How many immediate subordinates have you selected in the past two years? How did you go about it? Any surprises or disappointments?
19. How many immediate subordinates have you removed from their jobs in the last few years? Any contemplated? One example of how you went about it.
20. How do you feel your subordinates would describe you as a delegater? Any deliberate tactics you use?
21. Some managers keep a very close check on their organization. Others use a loose rein. What pattern do you follow? How has it changed in the last few years?
22. What has been the most important surprise you have received from something getting out of control? Why did it happen?
23. Let's talk about standards of performance. How would you describe your own? What would your subordinates say? What would your boss say?
24. Sometimes it is necessary to issue an edict to an individual or the entire staff. Do you have any recent examples of edicts you have issued? Probe: Reasons? Results?
25. What things do you think contribute to your effectiveness as a supervisor?
26. From an opposite viewpoint, what do you think might interfere with your effectiveness as a supervisor?
27. In what respects do you feel you have improved most as a supervisor during the last few years?
28. What kind of supervisor gets the best performance out of you?
29. Some managers are quite deliberate about such things as communications, development, and motivation. Do you have any examples of how you do this?

30. What have you done about your own development in the last few years?
31. Would you describe your relationship with your last three supervisors?
32. Considering your relationships both inside and outside the component, would you give me an example of how you have been particularly effective in relating with others.
33. Would you also give me an example of how you might not have been particularly effective in relating with others.
34. Some people are short fused and impatient in their reactions. How would you describe yourself?
35. Have you encountered any health problems? What do you do about your health?
36. Most of us can look back upon a new idea, a new project, or an innovation we feel proud of introducing. Would you describe one or two such innovations you are particularly proud of?
37. How do you feel about your progress (career-wise) to date?
38. What are your aspirations for the future? Have these changed?
39. We sometimes compare the assets and limitations of our products with competition. Let's do a related thing with your career. Thinking of your competition for jobs to which you aspire, what would you say are your limitations? (Get three or more assets and three or more limitations.)
40. Are there any conditions of personal business, health, or family which would limit your flexibility for taking on a new assignment?

▶ Section III

1. Tell me about your present job.
2. Tell me about yourself.
3. What do you spend most of your time on in your job?
4. How do you feel about your present job?
5. What frustrates you about your job?
6. What do you think about your present employer?
7. Where do you rank your present job with other jobs you've held? Why?
8. How many hours a day do you think a person should spend on his job?
9. What do you feel is an acceptable attendance record?
10. Do you arrive at work on time?
11. What do you think about your supervisor?
12. What do you think are your supervisor's strengths? Weaknesses?

13. How does your supervisor treat others in your department?
14. What are your goals?
15. Where do you want to be professionally in ten years?
16. How much money do you expect to be making in ten years?
17. What is unique about yourself?
18. What have you done that indicates you are qualified for this job?
19. What do you think about [insert a current event of some controversy like the abolition of the death penalty]?
20. What can I do for you?
21. Do you have any questions?

Appendix B

EVALUATION FACTORS USED BY INTERVIEWERS

    This appendix consists of two sections. The first is a list of negative factors evaluated by interviewers reported by 153 companies surveyed by the Northwestern Endicott Report and which may lead to rejection. The second section is an evaluation sheet used by the trainee program of a major American bank.

▶ Section I

1. Poor personal appearance.
2. Overbearing—overaggressive—conceited "superiority complex" —"know-it-all."
3. Inability to express himself clearly—poor voice, diction, grammar.
4. Lack of planning for career—no purpose and goals.
5. Lack of interest and enthusiasm—passive, indifferent.
6. Lack of confidence and poise—nervousness, ill-at-ease.
7. Failure to participate in activities.
8. Overemphasis on money—interest only in best dollar offer.
9. Poor scholastic record—just got by.
10. Unwilling to start at the bottom—expects too much too soon.
11. Makes excuses—evasiveness—hedges on unfavorable factors in record.
12. Lack of tact.
13. Lack of maturity.
14. Lack of courtesy—ill mannered.
15. Condemnation of past employers.
16. Lack of social understanding.
17. Marked dislike for school work.
18. Lack of vitality.
19. Fails to look interviewer in the eye.
20. Limp, fishy handshake.
21. Indecision.
22. Loafs during vacations—lakeside pleasures.

23. Unhappy married life.
24. Friction with parents.
25. Sloppy application blank.
26. Merely shopping around.
27. Wants job only for short time.
28. Little sense of humor.
29. Lack of knowledge of field of specialization.
30. Parents make decisions for him.
31. No interest in company or in industry.
32. Emphasis on whom he knows.
33. Unwillingness to go where we send him.
34. Cynical.
35. Low moral standards.
36. Lazy.
37. Intolerant—strong prejudices.
38. Narrow interests.
39. Spends much time in movies.
40. Poor handling of personal finances.
41. No interest in community activities.
42. Inability to take criticism.
43. Lack of appreciation of the value of experience.
44. Radical ideas.
45. Late to interview without good reason.
46. Never heard of company.
47. Failure to express appreciation for interviewer's time.
48. Asks no questions about the job.
49. High pressure type.
50. Indefinite response to questions.

▶ Section II

Businesslike Appearance   Yes _____   No _____

Poise/Self Confidence   1 - 2 - 3 - 4 - 5 - 6 - 7 - 8 - 9 - 10

Maturity   1 - 2 - 3 - 4 - 5 - 6 - 7 - 8 - 9 - 10

Attitude/Enthusiasm   1 - 2 - 3 - 4 - 5 - 6 - 7 - 8 - 9 - 10

Verbal Communication Skills   1 - 2 - 3 - 4 - 5 - 6 - 7 - 8 - 9 - 10

Supervisory Potential   1 - 2 - 3 - 4 - 5 - 6 - 7 - 8 - 9 - 10

Alertness/Perceptiveness   1 - 2 - 3 - 4 - 5 - 6 - 7 - 8 - 9 - 10

Motivation/Initiative   1 - 2 - 3 - 4 - 5 - 6 - 7 - 8 - 9 - 10

Expressed Career Interest   1 - 2 - 3 - 4 - 5 - 6 - 7 - 8 - 9 - 10
    in Banking

Related Experience   1 - 2 - 3 - 4 - 5 - 6 - 7 - 8 - 9 - 10
    Background

Mobile within Region   Yes _____   No _____

EDUCATION:

    AIB Classes?   Yes _____   No _____

    College?   1yr.   2yrs.   3yrs

    4-Year Degree?   Yes _____   No _____

    Business Related?   Yes _____   No _____

    Major School?   Yes _____   No _____

PERFORMANCE RATING: Level 1 _____ Level 2 _____ Level 3 _____

I recommend this individual for the training program: Yes _____ No _____

COMMENTS:

INTERVIEWER _____

Name _____ Interviewed by _____

Address _____ Date _____

_____ Phone _____

High School _____ HIGHEST LEVEL:

Military or Work Experience _____ University _____

_____ Degree _____ Date _____

_____ Major _____

_____ Grades _____

_____ University _____

_____ Degree _____ Date _____

_____ Major _____

_____ Grades _____

_____ College Activities _____

_____ _____

General Remarks _____ _____

_____ _____

_____ _____

_____ Location Desired _____

_____ Best Suited for _____

_____ Salary Discussed _____

_____

_____ Referred by _____

_____ Screened by _____

_____

_____ _____

Approved for Commitment _____

INTERVIEWING FOR _____ REFERRED BY _____

■ Outstanding
— Below Standard Desired

	N/A	4	3	2	1	Considerations
BUSINESS LIKE APPEARANCE						
PERSONALITY						Congeniality, self-assurance, poise, tact attitude, maturity, judgment.
SELF-EXPRESSION						Grammar, clarity vocabulary, articulation, ability to communicate ideas
LEADERSHIP						Supervision (military work), elected offices, extracurricular activities.
DEMONSTRATED CAPACITY TO LEARN						Common sense, alertness, academic success, analytical ability, perceptiveness.
PARTICIPATION						Participation in activities, self-starter, energy level.
CAREER INTEREST IN BANKING						Knowledge and research into banking, background, interest, responsiveness, logical and complete inquiry, enthusiasm.

Overall Evaluation

_____ Recommend for Hire
_____ Do not Recommend for Hire
REMARKS:

Interviewer: _____

Signed: _____

Appendix C

QUESTIONS ASKED BY INTERVIEWERS WHEN THEY CHECK YOUR REFERENCES

An interviewee should be aware that a reference check may be made on him at some time during the interview process. These are some of the questions that may be asked. Numbers 8 and 9 are catch-alls. They can elicit responses relating to the candidate's moral character or other sensitive areas that an interviewer may not wish to query specifically. Number 10 is a method to get references from people not suggested by the interviewee. Interviewers recognize that an interviewee is not going to suggest as a reference one whom he knows will not give a good one. Therefore, by having the reference name some other references, the interviewer is getting to a more objective source—one who has not been preconditioned by the interviewee.

1. How long did he work for you?
2. What was the quality of his work?
3. How much responsibility did he have?
4. How did he get along with people?
5. Did he require close supervision?
6. Was he prompt?
7. Why did he leave your company?
8. Do you know of anything that would disqualify him for the job we're considering hiring him for?
9. Can you think of anything I should know about him that I haven't asked about?
10. Do you know anyone else to whom I could speak about him?

BIBLIOGRAPHY

Alvarez, Walter C., *Nervousness & Indigestion*. 3rd ed. Collier Books, 1967.

Ambrose, Stephen E. *The Supreme Commander*. Doubleday & Co., 1970.

Bach, George R., & Deutsch, Ronald M. *Pairing.* Avon Books, 1971.

Baker, Carlos. *Ernest Hemingway: A Life Story.* Charles Scribner's Sons, 1969.

Bellows, Roger M. *Employment Psychology: The Interview.* Rinehart & Company, 1954.

Birren, Faber. *Color in Your World.* Crowell-Collier, 1962.

Bolles, Richard Nelson. *What Color Is Your Parachute?* Ten Speed Press, revised every year.

Brooks, John. "The Fate of the Edsel." In *Great Business Disasters,* edited by Isadore Barmash. Ballantine Books, 1973.

Capra, Frank. *The Name above the Title.* Macmillan, 1971.

Carnegie, Dale. *How to Win Friends and Influence People,* Simon & Schuster, 1936.

Davies, Hunter. *The Beatles.* Dell, 1968.

Fast, Julius. *Body Language.* Pocket Books, 1971.

Fenlason, Anne F. *Essentials in Interviewing.* Harper & Bros., 1952.

Fraser, John Munro. *A Handbook of Employment Interviewing.* 3rd ed. Macdonald & Evans, 1954.

_____. *Employment Interviewing.* 4th ed. Macdonald & Evans, 1966.

Gallwey, W. Timothy. *The Inner Game.* Random House, 1974.

Griffith, Thomas. "Newswatch." *Time,* November 8, 1976.

Halberstam, David. *The Best and the Brightest.* Random House, 1969.

Harriman, W. Averell, and Abel, Ellie. *Special Envoy to Churchill & Stalin.* Random House, 1975.

Honig, Donald H. *Baseball: When the Grass Was Real.* Coward, McCann & Geoghegan, 1975.

Ivey, Paul W. *Successful Salesmanship.* 6th ed. Prentice-Hall, 1942.

Jameson, Robert. *The Professional Job Changing System.* 4th ed., rev. Performance Dynamics, 1976.

Lay, Beirne, Jr. *Someone Has to Make It Happen.* Prentice-Hall, 1969.

Lopez, Felix M., Jr. *Personnel Interviewing Theory and Practice.* McGraw-Hill Book Company, 1965.

Lundgren, Hal. "Injury Effects Still Plague Greene," *The Sporting News,* November 13, 1976.

Mahler, Walter R. *How Effective Executives Interview.* Dow-Jones-Irwin, 1976.

Maltz, Maxwell. *Psycho-Cybernetics.* Pocket Books, 1966.

Medley, H. Anthony. *UCLA Basketball: The Real Story.* Galant Press, 1972.

Nixon, H. K. *Principles of Selling.* McGraw-Hill Co., 1931.

Oldfield, R. C. *The Psychology of the Interview.* 4th ed. Methuen & Co., 1951.

Peale, Norman Vincent. *The Power of Positive Thinking.* Prentice-Hall, 1952.

Pogue, Forrest C. *George C. Marshall: Ordeal and Hope.* Viking Press, 1966.

Rapaport, Ron. "A Man Has to Fear What's Down the Road." *Los Angeles Times,* November 2, 1976.

Rickenbacker, Edward V. *Rickenbacker.* Prentice-Hall, 1967.

Schuller, Robert H. *Move Ahead with Possibility Thinking.* Fleming H. Revell, 1975.

Sorensen, Theodore C. *Kennedy.* Harper & Row, 1965.

Thomas, Bob. *Thalberg.* Doubleday, 1969.

Turnbull, Andrew, (editor). *The Letters of F. Scott Fitzgerald.* Charles Scribner's Sons, 1963.

Walters, Barbara. *How to Talk with Practically Anybody about Practically Anything.* Doubleday, 1970.

Weber, Eric. *How to Pick up Girls.* Bantam Books, 1971.

Weinland, James D., and Gross, Margaret V. *Personnel Interviewing.* Ronald Press Company, 1952.

Zunin, Leonard, with Zunin, Natalie. *Contact—The First Four Minutes.* Nash Publishing Company, 1972.

Index